CW01494964

Slightly Foxed Editions

MANGO AND MIMOSA

SLIGHTLY FOXED EDITIONS

No. 17

MANGO AND MIMOSA

Suzanne St Albans

First published by Slightly Foxed in 2012
in a limited edition of 2,000 copies
of which this is copy No.

1792

© The Estate of Suzanne St Albans 1974, 1976

Slightly Foxed Ltd
67 Dickinson Court
15 Brewhouse Yard
London ECIV 4JX

The moral right of the author has been asserted.
All rights reserved. Without limiting the rights under copyright reserved above, no part
of this publication may be reproduced, stored or introduced into a retrieval system, or
transmitted, in any form or by any means (electronic, mechanical, photocopying,
recording or otherwise), without the prior permission of both the copyright holder and
the publisher of this book.

A CIP catalogue record for this book is available from the British Library.

ISBN 978-1-906562-34-2

Printed by Smith Settle, Yeadon, West Yorkshire

Preface

Sometime in 1999 a light editing job dropped through my letterbox – 'a new edition of a memoir by the Duchess of St Albans', the publisher had said on the phone. Preparing myself for some gently rambling aristocratic reminiscence, I made a fresh cup of coffee and sat down to take a look.

Hours later I was still sitting there, entranced. I had never heard of its author, but from the first page of this magical memoir I knew I was in the company of a natural writer and a most unusual and lovable human being – someone with a sense of fun and adventure, and an affectionate eye for human (and animal) eccentricity. I constantly wanted to be reading bits out loud to whoever was around.

In some ways it is surprising that Suzanne St Albans – or Suzanne Fesq as she then was – learned to write at all, for her childhood was distinctly light on education. Her parents, both of French origin, had met in Malaya, where her father had inherited a plantation called Assam Java. But soon after the First World War this strangely assorted couple – she emotional, impulsive and sociable, he virtually a hermit who would hide in the basement when anybody called – were overcome with a longing to put down roots in France. So they took over an old farmhouse near the small town of Vence, at the foot of the Alpes-Maritimes, and named it Mas Mistral.

From then on the family – which included Suzanne's younger brother and sister and her father's old Swiss nurse Marie – moved restlessly back and forth between Malaya and the South of France.

Life with Marie, however, was an education in itself, for she was a passionate naturalist. The nursery shelves were packed with jars of pickled spiders and scorpions, and at Assam Java – where they were forbidden to run about upstairs since the house was riddled with termites (it eventually collapsed) – the ground floor was given over to an animal hospital, where an assortment of patients, with wings and legs bound in bandages and splints, received expert attention: 'Marie said that the proper way of preparing worms was to chew them up first and I actually saw her put this into practice herself when dealing with a baby owl who was being difficult about his food.'

A rescued stork, who enjoyed fielding the shuttlecock when they played badminton, usually joined them for elevenses, and on their daily forays with Marie into the jungle, Suzanne and her sister each held the hand of their devoted little household monkey, while John brought up the rear, pushing his pet hen Titi, tucked up in a doll's pram with her head on the pillow. Lizards nested undisturbed in the nursery keyhole, and a small ladder was used by Titi for climbing into the children's clothes cupboard where she laid her eggs.

Back in France, their father decided to open a bookshop in Vence. But he couldn't bear to sell the books – 'to sell anything would have broken up the collection. With a little badgering you could sometimes borrow one, but you were never, *never* allowed to pay.' Unfortunately, rather too many people 'forgot' to return the books they borrowed, and the cost of replacing them every few months became prohibitive, so the bookshop idea had to be shelved.

The evocation of both these childhood worlds is wonderfully fresh and vivid – the pulsating heat of Assam Java, where strange creatures peered down from the palm thatch above the children's heads at night and 'frequently crashed to the floor with a thud and a squelch', the holiday expeditions to Bukit Fraser, a hill station where 'huge warm clouds of steam rolled out of the jungle, and the air was so sodden with mist you could almost scoop up the moisture in your hands'; the dreamy garden created by her parents at Mas Mistral, with its vine terraces, overloaded strawberry beds, peach, fig, pear, cherry, pomegranate and persimmon trees, and its convivial if eccentric household – almost as big as the one in Malaya, what with Rubio the houseman, a Spanish Basque with 'bright red hair and bright red political views', 'Pauvre Claire' the depressed housemaid, who had a 'forehead all crinkled with worry and a mouth pursed up like a hen's bottom', and others, alas too numerous to mention.

Equally vivid is the author's description of her relationship with Jacques, the son of a family who became the focal point of their annual holidays at St Georges, a little resort on the Atlantic coast – ecstatic summers on white beaches that 'started at the Spanish border and reached uninterruptedly northwards for hundreds of miles' – an idyll marred only by the dreaded gym lessons their mother insisted they take with a martinet called M. Dupont. By the time war threatened in 1939, Suzanne was becoming a young woman, and Jacques was beginning to want a different kind of relationship.

The German Occupation scattered the two families to the winds, with the Fesqs – who for complicated reasons had British passports – fleeing to England, forced to abandon Marie in France. Meantime their father was marooned in South-east Asia, where he spent most of the war in a prison camp. It was the end of Suzanne's childhood, and the point at which this story ends.

I met the late Duchess briefly only once, when she was in her eighties, but I learned from her obituaries that during the war she had worked in Psychological Warfare as a news writer in North Africa and Italy, and then in 1945 in Austria where she met and fell in love with the amusing and dashing Colonel Charles Beauclerk. When he finally inherited the dukedom (at birth he was only ninth in line), it came with a string of titles, including that of Grand Falconer of England, but very little else. In an effort to recoup the family fortunes he embarked on an ill-advised business career which foundered spectacularly and ignominiously in 1973, and lost virtually everything.

So he and the Duchess retired to Mas Mistral where, in her usual spirited way, she took up her pen and produced this memoir – partly, presumably, in the hope of making some money, and partly perhaps to recapture some of that happy lost childhood world – as well, apparently, as 'five other non-fiction books' which I have been unable to trace. Not bad for someone whose first language was French, and who never

seems to have gone to school for more than a year at a time –
though perhaps that was her saving grace, for she retained a
youthful enthusiasm and freshness which permeate this funny
and original book. She was certainly quite a gal.

HAZEL WOOD

This book is dedicated to the three most dauntless people I have ever known – my father, my mother and Marie

Part I

MANGO AND MIMOSA

1922–1930

I

Soon after the First World War, when I was twelve months old, my parents, who shared a nebulous but incurable longing for roots and close contact with the soil, bought an old farmhouse which went with a strip of land on a hillside near the small town of Vence, at the foot of the Alpes-Maritimes in Provence, and set about making it into a family home. When it was finished they called it 'Mas Mistral' – after the poet, not the wind.

The ground floor, where the farmer and his donkey had bedded down together, became the dining-room, while a flight of outside stone steps led to the first floor. The cooking was done on a charcoal fire out of doors. Old Provençal tiles covered the roof, and the thick walls and small square windows ensured a cellar-like coolness in the hottest months, while an enormous fireplace, in which half an olive tree could burn away happily, kept the dining-room warm and cosy in the winter. The iron ring to which the donkey had been tied remained in its place, and is still there to this day.

With a gang of builders, masons, carpenters and plumbers and a fleet of ancient lorries, my father began his building operations. In contrast to the shaky, wobbly constructions in which he had lived in Malaya (later, at Assam Java, Papa's

Malayan estate, we were forbidden to run on the first-floor landing in case the house should collapse on top of us), this one was to be built, literally, on rock. And he dug until he found it. Huge foundations were excavated and great stones three feet thick were hacked out of the mountainside and used for the walls. Papa wanted to make sure this house wouldn't wobble. And so preoccupied was he with indestructibility that all architectural charm and grace were forgotten, and the house that rose from the ground was square, plain and unattractive – but infinitely durable.

The new house, the plans for which had been drawn up by my father, was tacked on to the old farm, and doors were pierced through the wall on two floors. How Papa managed to devise anything so complicated defies understanding, and makes description difficult. However much I puzzle over it, and scrutinize the building both from the inside and the out-side, I fail to understand how the various levels fit in and join up together. There is no front door, or perhaps you could say there are four front doors.

After the Second World War when my parents returned to Mas Mistral, and they were living there alone without staff, they felt the need, goodness knows why, to build on a new wing facing east. A third central heating plant was installed so that, on very cold days, all three could be heard thrumming, rumbling and hissing together, turning the house into a fur-nace. But in spite of this greenhouse temperature, Papa, whose blood had been thinned by fifty years in the tropics, still crept around with a shawl over his shoulders and an anxious look on his face, muttering 'The water will freeze in the pipes if it doesn't warm up soon!' as he tapped the glass of the thermometer on the wall.

The furniture, which my parents had collected from farmhouses and village shops far and wide, was antique Provençal, beautifully made and quite unobtainable nowadays. Everywhere, in all the rooms, were priceless Chinese and Japanese vases and silver objects, all collectors' pieces, which I found perfectly hideous.

My parents' weak spot was pictures. Apart from Papa's own oils and water-colours dotted about here and there, there were none except a few Japanese prints hung from the picture rails high up near the ceiling. But to make up for this lack, there were hundreds of photographs from all parts of the world, going back to the 1850s and '60s, in silver frames everywhere.

Underneath the house and scooped out of the mountainside was the cellar, where in due course the grapes were crushed in a great vat at the time of the *vendange*; and the barrels in which the juice boiled and bubbled until it turned to wine stood in rows like Ali Baba's jars. Until very nearly the end of his life, Papa spent whole days down there, presumably quite happy, bottling and decanting, sticking on labels and hiding away from visitors.

At the top of the house, under the roof, was a huge attic which could easily have been made into a large and comfortable flat. This was our favourite place, stuffed with treasures of every kind, and full of ghosts and rats and enormous lizards which crashed about in fearful midnight battles over our heads. And as a background to all this, there were continual orchestral effects of sighing and rattling, and mysterious gurgling sounds. We were never allowed up there alone, which naturally added to its fascination and attraction.

Along the whole front of the house ran a balcony, which was soon festooned with bignonia, wisteria and moonflowers climbing up from the terrace below, so that for six months of the year at least the whole front was covered with thick clusters of flowers. The bignonias were always obscured by a thick coating of ants, which were so addicted to the flowers' heady juices that they came hurrying from miles around as soon as the plants began to bloom.

Ants were an all-year-round plague. When on the move, marching sixteen abreast in close formation, they would take short cuts through the house to gain time and save their legs, and you would come across their columns at all hours of the day in the most unlikely places. When their journey happened to take them through the larder, whole legs of lamb and sides of pork would disappear overnight, leaving pink bare bones, and pots of home-made jam were sucked dry and left smooth and gleaming on the shelves. '*Ces sacrées fourmis!*' Marie, our nanny, would splutter as she followed their trail, pumping furiously at her 'Fly-tox' gun and spraying everything in sight. The ants, needless to say, were not in the slightest bit incommoded. But their greatest addiction of all, electricity, fortunately polished them off by the thousand. Swarming into the wall plugs, they clustered there in a drugged stupor, and had to be scraped out with nail-files and meat skewers. (Once, when wanting to do some ironing in the kitchen after the war and finding the plug bunged up with electrocuted ants as usual, I started to scratch away at them with a hairpin, the whole thing exploded in my face, and I was thrown flat on my back on the floor.)

While the new house was being built, we all camped very comfortably in the old farmhouse, known locally as Le Vieux Mas – my parents, my new-born brother John, who lived in one of those tall gangling prams all made of wire and trembling springs which shuddered in the slightest breeze, myself now aged about 2, and Marie, who had joined us from Australia. Marie had brought Papa up in Sydney, where he had been born thirty-five years before, and now she had answered his appeal to come and look after his young family.

All that first summer, while the house was growing, clouds of dust hovered in the hot, still air. The workmen, bare to the waist and with wide red cummerbunds around their middles, churned miles of sand and cement, ran up and down scaffolding and made a great deal of noise. And all through the night, under constant very white moonlight, clouds of fireflies swarmed over the land as far as the eye could see, while a chorus of frogs kept up their monotonous croaking until dawn, when the cicadas and the birds took over for the daylight hours.

To get me quickly to bed on those hot scented evenings, when everything in the garden called you irresistibly out of doors, Marie told me that I would be turned to stone if the moon ever caught sight of me with my pants down. And so for a long time I refused to undress to go to bed, thereby causing a great deal more trouble and defeating Marie's original object.

2

Both my great-grandfathers, born within a year of each other in Bordeaux, set off more or less at the same time to explore the world in different directions, little knowing that their grandchildren, my parents, would meet and marry in Malaya seventy years later.

Great-Grandfather Fesq, on my father's side, settled in Australia in 1848, after having spent a few years sailing to and from New Orleans with shiploads of wine which he sold there at good profit. He had run away from home at the age of 15 after his father's death, on the suspicion that his mother, and the doctor whom she married very soon after, had done his father in. And there may have been something in it, as his uncles, with whom he sought asylum in Bordeaux, made no attempt to send him back, but instead gave him a job in their wine-exporting business.

After a few profitable years on the New Orleans run, Great-Grandpapa fell in love with a cotton planter's daughter. As the moons of her fingernails were too dark to denote pure white ancestry, he begged to be allowed to take his cargo to the other end of the world, as mixed marriages 'weren't done' in those days. His uncles obligingly consented to this, so from then on French claret was dispatched to Sydney instead of New

Orleans. After a few years he bought land, including a good chunk of what is now Sydney Harbour, built several villas, married and begat a family, and there have been Fesqs there ever since.

While Great-Grandfather Fesq was busily plying his trade between Bordeaux and New Orleans, his opposite number, Great-Grandfather Chasseriau, had landed in Mauritius, where he spent a few years planting sugar cane. But soon, feeling hemmed in by the diminutive size of the island, he set off again across the seas, and this time landed in Malaya. And the Chasseriaus remained there for the next hundred years.

After I was born, my parents decided to come to Europe and re-establish a permanent home in France. As my mother was a British subject through the accident of her birth in Penang, a Crown colony at the time, and Papa was Australian, they regarded themselves as part of the British colonization of the South of France, which was then in full swing.

Mamma, whose veins flowed with good, red, pugnacious Gallic blood, was nonetheless fanatically devoted to England, the Empire and all things British. This completely prejudiced and unreasoning attitude remained with her to the end of her days, and nothing got her French blood up so much as the slightest criticism of England – even its weather she considered the best in the world. But Papa, who knew better, insisted on the sun.

* * *

Marie had first joined my father's family when he was 3 years old. His mother had originally discovered the 20-year-old on one of her many trips to Europe, and brought her home to Sydney as nanny to her children. There is a photograph of the young Marie, with leg-of-mutton sleeves and wasp waist, but without the gold-rimmed spectacles to which she took soon after. Her hair, which remained pale shining gold until her death and was never cut, was always scraped severely back from her face. Although she was of peasant stock, there was a look of great elegance and breeding about her.

An accident with a merry-go-round had left Marie with only one good eye. She had taken my father and his brother and sister to a local fairground, where she hoisted them on to the wooden horses, then stood back to watch. At that moment a spark from the coal-powered engine fluttered into her left eye, boring right through the bright-blue pupil and destroying the optic nerve. I still have those fierce gold-rimmed spectacles with lenses no bigger than shelled almonds, which scored a deep groove into the bridge of her nose as she hardly ever took them off, even on occasion going to bed wearing them. Handicapped though she was, she could still see as well as most people with two good eyes in their heads. Moreover, she could see right through people, and claimed that many of them had such murky souls that they left a dark stain on their surroundings.

When my father and his brother and sister reached their teens, Marie had gone to Switzerland for her first holiday in sixteen years, and married a widowed policeman with four-teen children. Some of them, she told us, had been difficult at first, but she soon had them eating out of her hand. Eventually she had a son of her own, who died of meningitis when only a few months old. He was a beautiful baby. The photograph of his little corpse, all draped in satin ribbon, lace and paper roses, hung between our beds in the night nursery. On the anniversary of his death, the picture would be taken down, a candle lit in front of it, and we would all kneel around it weeping at Marie's grief and the terrible sadness of it all, and praying for the repose of his little soul.

Her husband had died soon after the baby, and my grand-mother had no difficulty in persuading Marie to return to Australia. And when, in the course of time, Papa wrote asking her to come and look after his growing family in Vence, she came and stayed until the Second World War scattered us to all parts of the globe.

Marie worshipped my father, and I suspect that she may have been the first and perhaps the greatest love of his life. They often conferred together in German, in low confidential voices, and the impression we got was that they were com-plaining about my mother. Whenever there was a crisis it was Marie my father turned to, not my mother. I am quite sure that the relationship was an innocent one, and that they were unaware themselves of anything more than the perfectly nor-mal bond of trust and affection which habitually existed in those days between master and servant. I have a photograph of Papa as a boy, looking like a Proustian character, with one large and bony hand lying in Marie's lap, while a smug and unconsciously revealing smile plays on her face. Although she may not have been completely aware of the influence that she had over him, the smile certainly indicates some inkling of it.

But when, not long after her arrival at Mas Mistral, my new-born brother John was placed in her arms, he took possession of her heart altogether, so that the vague indifference she had felt for me until then became more marked and I fell out of favour entirely. Perhaps she saw him as the reincarnation of her own son. It made no difference whatever to my devotion to her, and I would bend over backwards to win a smile, swallowing great lumps of gristle, feeding bits of chocolate to John, which he dribbled all over his clothes, and sticking dandelions and daisies in his ears to make him look like those lovely pigs' heads I so admired in the butchers' shops, with their nostrils bristling with tufts of parsley. I even walked ostentatiously *round* puddles instead of splashing straight through them, as I longed to do. All to no avail – my efforts were simply dismissed as 'showing off'.

Soon John was joined by my sister Anne, who appeared quite suddenly in Marie's arms one April day when the palm trees were being pruned and the terrace was child-deep in razor-sharp sword-like fronds. Having had no forewarning of the new arrival, we stared at this creature in amazement. I was most struck by her fingers, of which she had a complete if minute set on each hand. This *was* a discovery, for babies, I firmly believed, grew like tadpoles in reverse, adding new bits as they grew older instead of dropping them off. But John remained Marie's favourite – after all, he was my father's son, and we were my mother's daughters.

Marie's relations with Mamma, whom she openly disliked and despised, were bad from the start. Their mutual jealousy, of which they were probably unaware, was always aggravated when my father was at home. A sort of truce, uncertain but welcomed by us with relief, reigned when he was away. Another cause of friction was Mamma's impulsiveness and lack of emotional control, which exasperated Marie, who regarded such 'weakness' as a lack of character.

Although strong on discipline, particularly where Anne and I were concerned, Marie allowed us a great deal of freedom. For the best part of the day we were in the garden, out of her sight and very often out of hearing as well. And during those hours of bliss, without lessons or obligations of any kind, when we did as we pleased, Marie filled her time reading French, German and English newspapers. For our benefit she marked paragraphs of special interest, way above our heads, and these she would read to us in the evening. It could be on any subject – science, politics, aviation, motor-racing or any current event that featured in the press at the time. As we knew neither English nor German, we found it all extremely boring. But Marie maintained that the best way to learn a language was to read the papers. The rest would come in due course. And because of this addiction to the press, she was incredibly well informed.

But overriding everything else was her passion for animals and for natural history. Every morning after breakfast she staggered out of the kitchen with heavy crocks of milk for the local cat population. Then she fed the birds that came sailing down from the trees to peck biscuits out of her hand and sit on her hat. In the evening, when she wasn't reading the newspapers aloud to us, we cleared everything away and helped her to press the plants we had collected on our walks. There were usually a few spiders, scorpions and various other fascinating creatures as well, to pickle or bottle for her insect collection lined up on the nursery shelves.

When she was in a particularly good mood, Marie would tell us stories of her childhood in Switzerland, of her grandmother who had stood by the roadside watching Napoleon and his army trekking over the mountains on their way to fight in Italy. Of her wise, far-sighted father, who predicted a time when carriages would zoom around the streets without any horses to pull them along. We never grew tired of her tales of life high in the Swiss Alps, of the autumn festivals when the cows, decked out in all the flowers of the mountains, came down in long processions from the high pastures, to be tucked up for the winter in the stable under the house. On those occasions dancing went on all night, with the lads slapping their heels and throwing the girls high in the air. Years later, in Malaya, during our jungle walks, when carried away by the poignant glory of her memories, Marie would sometimes break into a yodel, startling the monkeys in the trees above into stunned silence.

* * *

With Marie to look after us, our parents were able to get down to making the garden, planting fruit-trees, and laying out the vineyards and the strawberry beds. Their longing for roots must have been gratified at last, but when all this began to bear fruit, there was far more than the household could absorb.

The top of the garden, laid out in several terraces behind the house, was planted with vines. For the *vendange*, all hands were put to work. It was a period of delicious excitement, feverish activity and merrymaking. Memories of ancestral rituals stirred the peasants, and the whole of October was dedicated to grape-picking and wine-making. Neighbours lent their presses and helped to tread down one another's grapes. When we were old enough we were allowed to take part in this intoxicating exercise, and the feeling of the fat grapes squelching between our toes was infinitely satisfying.

Equipped with secateurs and old kitchen scissors, the neighbouring farmer and his friends who were helping with our harvest would start picking at sunrise, with hods strapped to their backs. We joined them after a hastily swallowed cup of cocoa as the early morning haze hovered over the vineyard, promising a fine day. Dragging baskets as large as ourselves, we snipped and tugged at the heavy grapes all through the day. It was a backbreaking job, as the largest bunches were usually hidden under the leaves low down on the vines, just clearing the ground. When the baskets were full, we staggered with them to the end of the row and tipped them into wheel-barrows, which were then trundled away to the cellar for the final crushing in the great wine vat.

The vine terraces were separated by sloping banks on which grew thousands of strawberry plants. We were allowed to help with the picking, and so gorged ourselves that we were invariably sick before the end of the day. Quantities were given away, and the rest went into sticky jams, cakes, puddings and tarts, until the smell of hot strawberry practically oozed out of the walls. Peach trees and greengages grew among the vines, while dotted here and there haphazardly were fig, pear, cherry, pomegranate and persimmon trees. On either side of the entrance to the old farmhouse, our parents planted avocados and tree-tomatoes, which were fed daily with doses of tea-leaves.

The garden in front of the house was devoted to mimosas, oleanders, palms and exotic plants from Malaya, China and Japan. From time to time, and for no apparent reason, Mamma would suddenly descend upon a bed of Chinese lilies, bamboo orchids or Cherokee roses, root the whole lot up and put down rows of string beans, pumpkins or tomatoes. She had probably been given the seeds by a neighbour, and having no other space available, she would ruthlessly sacrifice some of these exotic treasures without a second thought. Papa, suddenly coming across an outrage of this kind, would lift up his thin voice and bleat with distress: '*Mon dieu, mon dieu,* what has happened here? What vandalism! *Quelle horreur!*' Whereupon Marie, hearing his lamentations, would come hurrying out of the house to comfort him, muttering dark things about my mother in German.

One fine day in early spring, soon after Mas Mistral was finished, a large building suddenly began to rise on the hill behind us, on the very frontiers of our land. Marching off to Vence to see the Mayor, my mother learned that it was to be a sanatorium for TB patients. There was outrage in the family, for it had been done in a sly and underhand way, without warning of any kind. Fury was followed by consternation. Safe, as they thought, in having found a dry and healthy spot on which to build their house and rear their young, our parents felt truly cheated. Clouds of germs would now drift downhill on the breeze, pollute the air around us, and settle on our lungs, infecting us all with the dreaded disease, for which there was then no cure.

When the first patient arrived, we were bundled off to Nice to have our lungs X-rayed. And from then on, this became a very boring twice-yearly routine. Soon Vence was crawling with coughing, spluttering strangers. Whenever we came across one of them on our walks, Mamma would command in a loud voice, 'Cover up your face and SPIT! And don't breathe until I tell you.' And Marie would drag us away to the other side of the street.

The area had been advertised as having the best climate in the world for TB. And in a ghoulish sense this was indeed true. In those days it was believed that lying in the sun all day long was the most effective treatment for tuberculosis, though it was in fact the quickest way of speeding up the patient's death. Business for undertakers was brisk, and the church bells tolled incessantly as one funeral followed another, the victims borne off to the graveyard in the old horse-drawn cemetery cart, all draped in lace and with black feathers fluttering in the breeze.

In the end word got round, Vence was regarded with increasing suspicion, and the sanatorium was eventually closed. It reopened later as a miners' rest home for those with a disease even more deadly than the last – but as this was caused by coal-dust, it couldn't be spread by germs floating down the hill.

* * *

John was growing into a plump and rosy child, satisfactory in every way, and the most beautiful creature I had ever seen next to a new-born chick. But I was becoming difficult, and was full of tiresome fads and dislikes. Although I loved bees, I could *not* stand the taste or even the smell of the revolting honey they produced. This was the cause of endless strife, for Mamma was convinced that honey was a cure for all ills. And John, of course, lapped it up.

Milk was another problem. One of our neighbours was a farmer, who lived in incredible squalor in one room with his cow, his wife and hens, and a clutch of wild, retarded children. It was he who brought his milk every evening to our kitchen door. The poor man was riddled with syphilis (one of his ears had dropped off) and as his cow was certain to have TB, the milk had to be boiled almost solid to make it safe enough to drink. This produced clotted lumps of overcooked skin, which were added to our cocoa every day, since Mamma was convinced it held special virtues, made children fat and kept winter colds away. The slimy curds made me sick every time I tried to swallow them.

This daily nightmare ended when the unhappy farmer went down to the railway line in the valley and had himself run over by our little local train. The tragedy saddened the neighbourhood, but for me life looked up at once. My mother, who never wasted any time, promptly built a cottage at the bottom of the garden and imported a clean-living farmer and his wife, a beautiful shining cow, a mule, a donkey and a pig. The mule, who was never seen to do a day's work, spent his time rolling about in the grass. The donkey jogged us blissfully up and down the garden, and the pig went the way of all pigs. But most crucial of all was that the new cow's milk passed all the tests, and didn't have to be boiled solid any longer.

Madame Rose, the farmer's wife, very soon took control of our kitchen. She was a large bundly creature always dressed in layers of black skirts, and I loved to watch her at the kitchen range in her long white apron and black straw hat anchored to her bun with jet hairpins. She was at it all day long, concocting delicious stews and pâtés and delectable things out of pigs' ears, bladders and other unmentionable organs. She used everything that grew in the garden, and the store-cupboards were soon crammed with quince, strawberry and redcurrant jelly, raspberry and cherry jam, olives in brine, bottled peaches and pears, sugared plums and chestnuts, and prunes and raisins dried on little wire trays in the sun. Her cassis, plum, apricot and cherry brandy was made with *eau-de-vie* from Papa's vines. In the summer she would sit on the kitchen steps under the two orange trees with her lap spread out, surrounded by pots and pans of every kind and baskets filled with fruit. It was fascinating to watch her flicking stones out of the cherries with a hairpin – a useful trick which I was never able to master. But years later, in Vienna after the war, when faced with the austere rations of the British army, I taught myself to cook by trying to recreate the delicious smells which Madame Rose used to produce in our kitchen.

'Pauvre Claire', the little housemaid, mooned around the house with a feather duster and spent her afternoons pressing our clothes with a huge iron shaped like a camel's hoof and filled with live charcoal. From time to time she opened a trapdoor at the back and spooned in some more. It was Pauvre Claire who made the hens tipsy one day by throwing them handfuls of cherrystones which Madame Rose had soaked in *eau-de-vie* to make cherry brandy. Dazed out of their minds, they rolled over on their backs with their legs sticking straight up in the air. But as far as I remember, there were no lasting effects after they recovered from their massive hangover.

Pauvre Claire lived in a world of her own, and it was difficult to make friends with her. My mother had some natty dresses and stunning little caps made for her, but she remained uninterested. Her hold on life was too tenuous. She was to fade away only a few years later when she was barely 30.

Soon a couple of gardeners were added to the workforce.

They dug the heavy clay soil and looked after the vines, the strawberries and the fruit-trees. The flowers, which seemed to come up spontaneously, managed to grow by themselves, with scarcely any attention.

Gino, the older of the two, was tall and thin, with a bandage over his left ear and another across his right eye (syphilis again), which gave him a roguish air. He spoke a mixture of Italian patois and Provençal, which was perfectly clear to us but sometimes perplexed Mamma. She would call out to one of us, '*Qu'est-ce qu'il veut dire?*' And the message was duly translated. Every day he brought a different child with him. He had a large assortment of these, all crippled and suffering from a variety of infirmities. The child of the day, whom he carried all the way up from the village on his back, was settled under an olive tree, with its poor twisted limbs set out as comfortably as possible. Then a bottle of wine was planted in the grass within easy reach, and throughout the day the little creature sucked away at it, crooning to itself in tipsy contentment.

Gino's colleague, Marius, was much younger, and still unmarried. Short and knotty, he was like a vine in winter when all the gnarls are showing. He came from Sardinia and spoke a curious brand of Southern Italian mixed with some of our local patois. We all understood him, more or less, except for Mamma, and Marie who pretended not to.

Another Italian who never troubled to learn any French was Caroline the washerwoman. A small hunchback with a handsome moustache, she screeched and cursed all day long as she whacked the sheets with an implement that looked like an old cricket bat. In summer the washing was done out of doors in two great stone troughs filled with cold water, one for soaping and the other for rinsing. Winter brought Caroline indoors where the laundry on the lower ground floor was equipped with the same stone troughs, and there she bashed and banged and cursed and screamed, with sprays of soapy water flying in all directions. Summer and winter the laundry was dried on the grass in the sun, where it acquired a delicious smell, a mixture of ozone and fresh grass which, when added to the verbena of the linen cupboards, gave the beds an unusual fragrance. For me, and despite everything that has happened since, this is still the signature smell of Mas Mistral.

The mattress woman came once a year, when spring-cleaning was in full swing. She set up her carding machine on the terrace under a cherry tree, and the mattresses were brought out to her one by one. Having unpicked them and pulled out all the flock, she would give the covers to Caroline to wash and then stuff the lumpy sheep's wool into her machine. After she had furiously pumped the handle back and forth for a while, the wool was all fluffed out like candy floss. Once washed and dried, it went back into the mattress, and she stitched it all together again with a needle the size of a dagger, which went right through to the other side, with small rounds of leather to protect the ticking from the sharp knots of string. When the mattresses were done, it was the turn of the carpets. They were tipped upside-down on the grass, beaten free of any remaining dust, then washed with vinegar, and finally fluffed up with damp tea-leaves.

The spring-cleaning of the attic was the last and most exciting phase of the operation. We talked about it for weeks beforehand, speculating on the treasures we would find. There were huge tea chests filled with old toys; tricycles and rocking horses stacked in corners, and everywhere quaint hats and old clothes for dressing-up, extraordinary shoes and Victorian button boots and parasols, Japanese kimonos, Chinese coolie hats, games of mahjong, tropical helmets and large leather cabin trunks labelled with names of long-distance P & O liners.

* * *

It was after spring-cleaning that the annual storms usually broke out. Apart from causing a good deal of damage to fruit-trees and vineyards, they were truly terrifying, especially when suddenly exploding over our heads after dark. Our eccentric lighting system would flicker on and off, and finally peter out altogether at the first flash of lightning.

All was well when Marie was there. In fact a good thunderstorm cracking over our heads, with her nodding at her newspaper by candlelight, was quite comforting. But once, when she had gone off to the dentist in Nice and Mamma's youngest sister was looking after us, a sudden storm broke over the house. Green lights flashed at the windows and we were plunged into instant darkness. Shocked by the unexpected fury of the outbreak, we panicked and became hysterical with fear. Our poor aunt, only 17 at the time and nearly demented herself, floundered around in the dark, feeling for matches, clattering into the furniture and yelling at us to shut up. The wind raged and howled around the house, and a shutter, broken loose from its moorings, banged against the wall like a battering ram.

To add insult to injury, when Madame Rose finally came in with our supper, *the wrong forks and spoons were laid on the table*. Instead of our own sets, engraved with our names, which we had used ever since we could remember, we were given huge grown-up silver, as heavy as garden tools. This was the last straw. We flatly refused to eat, driving those poor women mad until they found our own cutlery. When Marie eventually turned up, badly battered and soaked to the skin, she was so glad to be back that no punishment followed our disgraceful behaviour.

Next day a man came up from the village bearing a magnificent lightning-conductor, which he fixed to the highest chimney. As an extra precaution we handed him a celluloid angel, clad from head to foot in white samite (he belonged on top of the Christmas-tree), to attach to the lightning-conductor. And after this, every morning we would rush out to see how he was faring. His gleaming robe gradually turned from dazzling white to lemon-yellow, then light ochre, but he remained at his post until the next storm, when he took off, bearing away his lightning-conductor with him. We assumed the ordeal had been too much for him and that he had fled back to the safety of heaven, riding his mount like a witch on her broom.

3

When a rather eccentric cousin of my husband's once said to me that he had been getting on with his mother much better since her death, I thought he was being his usual loopy self. But now I realize that you don't even *know* your parents, let alone get on with them, until after their death. The relationship, which is inevitably blurred by long conditioning, doesn't clear until they are no longer there, and their eccentricities, so desperately embarrassing at the time, turn into harmless memories.

My mother's childhood had been spent in the country near Bordeaux, at the Château des Charmilles, with her two brothers and two sisters, under the autocratic rule of her paternal grandmother. The children were much left to the care of servants, and from all accounts it was not a happy childhood for any of them.

When Mamma was 17, she went out to Malaya to join her parents, and I believe that the next four years until her marriage were the happiest of her life. Her father had by then founded Alma Estate, which was a flourishing several-million-pound concern.

Grandpapa, who was a rumbustious extrovert, loved entertaining, and so numerous were the guests, and so unending the stream of people who came for dinner and stayed three weeks, that another bungalow – a visitors' annexe – had to be built in the garden to accommodate them. As the Chasseriaus also ran their own hospital for the benefit of their workmen, my grandmother must have welcomed the arrival and help of her eldest daughter.

According to the *Pinang Gazette*, she and Grandpapa were forever singing duets at charity concerts, and organizing balls and fancy-dress parties on every possible occasion. There were visits from the Governor, and receptions at the Sultan's Palace, where my grandfather made 'enthusiastic speeches' (which must have been excruciatingly embarrassing for his family). The *Pinang Gazette* described my mother as 'the prettiest girl of Province Wellesley'.

I have never been able to discover how or where she met my father, or how those two human beings, so totally different in every way, could ever have thought they would find happiness together. My father plunged his bride immediately into solitude and loneliness through his relentless discouragement of all entertaining and hospitality. But somehow she kept herself going and her spirits bubbled on for many years, although it must have been very hard for her to be married to a hermit. They say that opposites attract each other, but surely in this case it was a matter of extremes.

My mother was straightforward, honest and transparent as a sheet of Perspex, and completely incapable of dissimulation, lying or any kind of pretence whatsoever. Everything came straight out, sometimes to our shame and misery, so that we treacherously disowned her whenever we could, clinging to Marie, whose reactions were so much more predictable. With Marie at least you could be pretty certain that whatever happened and whatever the circumstances, she would be harsh and severe, so that you usually had time to prepare yourself for whatever was coming.

Not so with Mamma. Catching you out at some wholly absorbing occupation – such as puncturing a tube of tooth-paste with a set of neat little pin-holes, or carefully picking out the yellow centres of marguerites while leaving the petals intact – would drive her into a frenzy of rage. Not only would she revile you for the present crime, but this would remind her of all your past offences, which she hurled at you with mount-ing fury, as the enormity of your misdeeds built up in her mind. One moment she was in a cheerful and jovial mood, and seconds later she might be screaming at you and chasing you out of the room with the most fearful imprecations. When I was about 7 and she tried hard to teach me to read, most lessons ended in tears, while I was accused of deliberately doing my best to exasperate her. It was greatly to her credit that she eventually broke through my mental block and I was able to read at last. But it was a severe trial, and we were both on the verge of a nervous breakdown by the end of it.

On the whole Mamma was always much happier in England and Malaya than in France. Unable ever to master the English language properly, she was nevertheless insanely prejudiced in favour of everything British. When she went into a London shop and someone spoke a word or two of

French to her, she was ecstatic with admiration at their perspicacity in guessing that she was French. She never tired of telling them how clever and wonderful they were and, not surprisingly, they adored her. It was a great pity that my father couldn't stand the climate, as I think they would have been much happier in England than in France.

When, in Vence, I accompanied my mother on her shopping expeditions, her behaviour sometimes filled me with embarrassment. She would race through the narrow streets, fight her way to the head of the throng (nobody ever queues in France), and to my amazement people made way for her with good humour. And then, in order to get from one street to another, she would take short cuts, diving straight through people's houses. Housewives looked up from their cooking pots, grandmothers peered up from the stockings they were knitting, children stood up from the table where they toiled at their homework and said *'Bonjour Madame'* as if it was the most natural thing in the world to have their home used as a right-of-way.

When my mother's father retired from Malaya, he built himself a house in Vence, which he called the Villa Ste Claire, but unfortunately he did not live to enjoy it for very long. Those colonials seem to have had no idea of architecture at all, for this house, though not quite as hideous as some of the monstrosities that disfigure the South of France, was pretty unattractive as well, although much improved by the palms and banana trees which were hastily planted all round. After it was finished, everybody realized that the less you saw of the house the better. But in spite of its inner and outer ugliness, it seemed like a paradise to us, as it was always running with dogs who were allowed *everywhere*. Nobody ever thought of turning them off the beds or the furniture.

It seemed that, unlike our own father, Grandpapa loved young people. Mamma, her brother Henri (who was very soon to die from the after-effects of being gassed in the war), her sister Isabelle and their friends danced all the afternoon, sang duets or opera at the piano, and went off to play endless games of tennis. Suzanne Lenglen, who was one of their gang, launched the fashion for white headbands, so that all the females blossomed out in them. Sometimes they all got into open cars and headed for the coast, or a place in the mountains called Peïra-Cava, to which for some mysterious reason they were continually repairing.

My father having returned to Malaya by then, and Mamma's spasmodic interest in our welfare being regarded as intolerable interference by Marie, who kept us jealously to herself, there was very little for Mamma to do except enjoy herself. And I am glad that she had the sense to do it.

For a short time Grandpapa was well enough to come up to Mas Mistral, and joke and chatter with us, then play the piano and sing with Mamma after we had gone to bed. We used to huddle at the top of the stairs to listen to their singing and their laughter and all the cheerful noises from which we were excluded. And I remember quite clearly the resentful sentence which went through my head at the top of those stairs: '*Ils dînent tard, ils chantent tard et ils rient toute la nuit.*'

After a few months, when summer was drawing to an end, poor Grandpapa was taken ill, wilted and died. We had never seen my mother cry before, and it was very upsetting. After she had left for the funeral, Marie dressed us all in white and walked us down to the village, where we took up our position outside the church. When the coffin had been loaded on to the hearse and the family, friends and neighbours had filed past, we tacked ourselves on to the end with the ragtag and bobtail of the town. Mamma, who had not wanted us to go, was very angry when she heard that Marie had taken us. It did not, however, have any traumatic effect on us. We had not known our grandfather well enough to be upset by his death, which we did not really understand anyway.

Besides, we knew and greatly admired *le corbillard*, with handsome black ostrich plumes waving on the roof, and enormous springs like hoops which creaked and groaned, particularly on the mountain paths and country lanes that had been deeply scored by the torrential winter rains. It was a familiar sight, toiling and bumping through the countryside, followed by a procession of mourners snaking slowly behind. We often saw the horses, which were black all over except for a white diamond-shaped patch on their foreheads, exercising the hearse between funerals. On duty, they were draped down to the ground in handsome black medieval-style coats embroidered with silver stars, and each proudly sported black ostrich plumes on his forehead. On the whole, therefore, far from being traumatized, we were proud to see our grandfather, dead though he was, riding in such glory.

At the cemetery, my mother and her female relations, all smothered in their weeds, stood at the gates shaking hands, as if receiving guests at a reception. When it was our turn to go to her own funeral, we could not find it in ourselves to follow her example and behave in such a civilized manner, and instead allowed 'the guests' to pile in helter-skelter, ungreeted at the gates.

* * *

One terrible day, when John must have been unusually provoking, Marie, who loved him more than anyone else on earth, having been brought to the boil by his naughtiness, gave him a good spanking. Taking him outside, she walloped his bottom with a slipper under the orange trees behind the kitchen. Overcome by the indignity of this treatment, he set up such an uproar that Mamma came hurrying out to see what was happening. The sight of John being spanked was so unusual that it must have taken her by surprise and thrown her off-balance. She shouted at Marie to stop at once, which order was naturally ignored, so that Mamma saw red and completely lost her temper.

'Put that child down,' she roared above the din, 'I forbid you to touch my son!' At this Marie dropped John like a hot potato and rounded on my mother. 'In that case, Madame, I will leave at once,' she said, in a voice like a corncrake. And she flounced into the house, barked at Marius to bring her trunk down from the attic, and rushed upstairs to her room.

Scooping up John from the grass where he had been dropped, I scrambled after her, both of us wailing and keening like banshees, begging her not to desert us. But the trunk was packed and lashed round and round with a stout rope and a variety of leather straps. Alerted (perhaps by Marius), the railway cart, pulled by the old railway horse, came lumbering up the hill, and the trunk was loaded on.

By then we were in a state of utter despair bordering on hysteria, and clung to Marie's skirts, begging her not to go. My mother had completely disappeared, and I have never discovered what her feelings were at the time. Was it dismay at the thought of losing Marie, or was it relief? In many ways it must have been intensely irritating for her never to be able to be mistress in her own household. Moreover, our devotion to Marie must have been galling, as we never made any fuss at all when Mamma went away. We knew, of course, that she would always return, although we were never informed whether it would be in a few days or a few months. And quite possibly, most of the time, she did not know herself.

Clutching at Marie's skirts and demented with grief, we sobbed and howled, when suddenly the coachman hopped off his perch and, shouting above the clamour, *'Voyons, Madame Marie, vous n'allez pas laisser ces gosses!'*, dragged her trunk off the cart and swung it on to the grass. Then, scrambling back on to his box, he turned the horse round and clattered off down the hill again. Marie's face was saved, and this, for us, most appalling of all disasters was averted. The trunk was duly lugged up to Marie's room again.

Shortly after this episode, my mother disappeared, and we learned later, by chance, that she had gone to Paris to build a house there. But thank goodness we were never made to go and live in it. Although we never saw it, photographs made it look perfectly hideous – a white box with a flat roof, it looked like a mausoleum.

* * *

The reverse side of Mamma's warm-hearted and hospitable nature was that her dislikes were as uncontrollable as her generous impulses. Many years later when we were all back at Mas Mistral with our husbands and assorted children, I dropped a brick which I shall never forget. The man who had rented D. H. Lawrence's house next door had, unbeknown to me, long been trying to infiltrate himself into our household. As I knew nothing about it, it seemed natural to invite him to tea when I met him in the village one day and he said how much he longed to see us all again.

Forgetting about it at once, I was surprised when he turned up the next day. We were all having nursery tea in the dining-room. My mother, seated in an armchair, had a grandchild on her knee, and eight or nine other small creatures were stuffing themselves with bread and jam at the table. As he minced in through the open door, our neighbour, bowing low, swept off his hat, saying how grateful he was for my kind invitation. My mother gaped at him in disbelief, and then exploded. Her fury took us all completely by surprise. She told him that he had no business to take advantage of my stupidity to worm his way into the house, that she had already told him that he was not welcome, and so would he please leave immediately. We were stunned by this outburst, and stared as the poor man turned tail and fled. Meanwhile, my mother had regained her composure and resumed her task of stuffing prunes and baked custard into the face of the baby on her lap.

After the war, when they retired from Malaya, my parents managed Mas Mistral without any live-in staff. Sometimes my father would go off for a whole month at a time to take a cure at Châtel-Guyon, leaving Mamma entirely on her own. Marvelling at her bravery in sleeping alone in that huge house, I asked her how she managed not to be nervous at night. Oh, she answered, there was no reason to be nervous, as a strange dog that she had never met before came to the kitchen door every evening and insisted on spending the night on guard by her bed. He departed in the morning after a bowl of tea (so good for their coats, you know) and returned punctually at nightfall. He never came while my father was there, but always reappeared during the 'cure' periods.

* * *

As he grew older, Papa's mania for solitude grew more marked, and if anybody threatened to pay us a visit he would exclaim, 'What does that idiot want to come here for? *We* don't want to see him,' and his agitation was such that the prospective visitor had to be put off as tactfully as possible. If anybody had the temerity to call without warning, he would dive into the cellar and remain there until winkled out, only emerging on the assurance that the offending caller was well off the premises.

We were really put on the spot on one occasion soon after my younger sister's wedding, when some of her new husband's friends, who had come all the way from England for the occasion, climbed up the hill to Mas Mistral to see Papa, as they had had no chance to talk to him at the reception. When he saw them panting up the garden path, he shot out of his chair and dashed to the door with unaccustomed velocity: 'Get rid of them,' he squeaked in petulant tones, as he beetled down to his cellar, 'I won't come out until they've gone.' So we had to tell the guests that he had gone up the mountain for a walk, and there was no knowing when he would be back. 'Oh never mind,' they said cheerfully, they were in no hurry and didn't mind waiting in the least. And so for two solid hours they sat and waited, while the family lunch scorched and turned black in the oven, and Papa fumed in the cellar. But he stuck it out until they gave up and went away.

He really should have been a monk, and I am quite certain that the happiest time of his life was the years that he spent in captivity in Singapore during the Second World War. His ascetic spirit yearned for austerity, and anything joyful and light-hearted seemed to him frivolous and worthless. Changi camp in the hands of the Japanese reduced life to basic essentials, and there he came face to face with absolute standards. In a monastery he could have achieved this state with the minimum of frustration, whereas out in the world he was constantly deflected, so that it was only through the horrors of a Japanese prisoner-of-war camp that he was able to get anywhere near his ideal. Once he had found it, the rest of his life, after his release, was nothing but a come-down from this higher state.

Above all, no emotional demands of any kind were made on him in captivity. These, I think, he dreaded above all else. Reserved and undemonstrative, he was terrified of our youthful, spontaneous affection. This had to be transformed into awe and veneration before he was able to take it. Although I am quite sure that he was fond enough of his children, he could not bear our demands for attention. Emotionally, he simply was not equipped to cope with them. Human relationships panicked him. The fact that as children we worshipped him as God on earth was a great embarrassment to him. Anne, who was always the least neurotic of us all, handled him with a lightness of touch which I envied but was unable to emulate. When she was 8, remarks such as 'I've just seen your wife in the garden. She was looking quite pretty,' made him smile, and filled me with admiration at her daring. It worked. But it had to come naturally. And so our great love for him was as much of a burden to us as it was an embarrassment to him – an unwanted commodity.

Quite incapable of small talk, he made a virtue of it and declared that 'Only fools chatter on when they have nothing to say.' Cultured and sensitive as he was, and with all his interests, he could have had a great many friends, but I believe that in the whole of his life he had only two.

His cousin, a painter called Edouard Goerg, whom he had known since childhood, had come to settle at Saillans, a hundred miles or so away on the other side of the department of the Alpes-de-Haute-Provence. Although they saw each other only two or three times a year when he came to Mas Mistral (nothing would persuade Papa to leave the house to visit him), it gave Papa a great deal of pleasure to know that his cousin was so relatively close. And Anne told me that when he heard of Goerg's death, he broke down and sobbed inconsolably, and never really recovered from the shock.

His other great friend, who survived him, was Henri Fauconnier, author of *The Soul of Malaya*. He was already a planter when my father arrived in the peninsula in search of adventure at the age of 18. Their interests were identical, and the friendship that sprang up between them lasted until Papa's death. From time to time, we spent holidays with Henri Fauconnier's gifted children, and Helène, his eldest daughter, became one of my dearest friends.

* * *

Once Mas Mistral had been built, and every inch of the garden was laid out and planted, the gardeners took over the daily weeding and general upkeep and there was nothing left for my father to do. Feeling the need for a new activity, he bought the freehold of a corner site on the Place du Grand Jardin in Vence, and made it into a bookshop. A short trip to

Paris furnished it with a magnificent collection of art books, all the dictionaries and Larousses imaginable and even, oh joy, a section for children. On that special shelf we found *White Fang*, *The Last of the Mohicans*, *Robinson Crusoe*, *Mon Petit Trott*, *Oliver Twist* and Aksakov's *Russian Childhood*. This last took possession of our souls and held us in thrall for many months. As soon as she had finished it, Marie had to start reading it again from the beginning.

The trouble with the shop was that my father could not bear to sell the books. When he was not actually reading he stood in a trance, in silent contemplation of the shelves. To sell anything would have broken up the collection – a kind of sacrilege. With a little badgering, you could sometimes borrow one, and if you happened to want it very badly, you simply forgot to return it. That was all right as far as it went. But you were never, never allowed to pay for it.

As might have been expected, the venture was not a success financially. As it turned out, too many people forgot to return the books they borrowed. Replacing them every few months was very expensive, and my mother eventually put her business foot down. Much against his will, my father was finally persuaded to sell the bookshop. It has gone through a dozen hands since then, but it still bears the name he gave it: the 'Librairie Ligurienne'.

After the bookshop came the buses. *Le Petit Train* travelled from Nice to Marseilles one day and returned the next. It stopped at Vence, and everywhere else, on the way. Apart from that, our only communication with the outside world was by donkey. To remedy this, my father had the idea of starting a bus service. He bought half a dozen of these monsters from Messrs Renault et Cie and put them into service. The *chauffeurs* were picked off tables at the Café de la Régence and press-ganged into the job.

It was enormous fun, not untinged with moments of terror, to go to Nice in one of Papa's buses. Scattering goats and sheep before us, we rattled down the mountainside on what was little more than a track in those days, so closely skirting the edge overlooking the valley that we often had to close our eyes in a desperate appeal for mercy to St Christopher. Having been seen by this much overworked saint safely down to the bottom, we would pass the cemetery at the foot of Haut-de-Cagnes. There we had to bury our noses in our handkerchiefs, as the local stench made the air unbreathable, though it probably came from the village rubbish dump next door and not from the dead rotting in their graves as we then supposed.

The bus was very accommodating, dropping people off all along the road, picking up baskets and letters, and making unexpected detours into side streets in Nice to oblige some elderly party whose feet were killing her. A notice behind the driver's head said *'Défence de parler au chauffeur'*, but nobody paid this little bit of officious nonsense any attention. Conversation was general and animated, and the driver took a leading part, conducting it with his hands and swivelling round in his seat from time to time to drive a point home. My father never travelled on his own buses. A taxi drove him to Nice whenever he had to go there.

In the evening, after a long and satisfyingly exhausting day spent in the shops, we repaired to the Café de l'Univers where Marie had a beer, and we restored ourselves with cocoa and croissants. The bus waited patiently until everybody was ready. Then we all piled in and exchanged the news of the day. The drive back into the mountains in the dark was never quite as frightening as the race downhill in daytime, although the spluttering and groaning of the motor made it sometimes seem unlikely that we would ever make it.

4

Great-Grandfather Chasseriau, when he landed in Malaya, had met an Englishman who, over a drink, sold him several thousand acres of jungle. Having picked up a partner on the way, Great-Grandpapa set off at once with a gang of men and elephants to clear his newly acquired property.

Pirates, alerted by the bush telegraph, were awaiting them by a bend in the river, and the poor partner, taken by surprise, was struck through the heart with a kris, and that was the end of his adventures. But Great-Grandpapa was ready with his pistol, and within a few minutes the corpses of the pirates were drifting down the river, escorted by a fleet of hungry crocodiles. Undeterred, he carried on with his pioneering alone, and from then on, continually called upon by the Rajahs of the surrounding states to restore order, he became, willy-nilly, the policeman of Northern Malaya, marching his battalion of armed men and elephants wherever a new war broke out.

This was before Henry Ridley had won his battle for rubber-planting in Malaya, and the wars between the invading Chinese and the local Malays over the tin mines were constant and fearful. Great-Grandpapa suppressed the bandits and administered justice, and if a few corpses were hanging from the surrounding trees by the end of the morning session, there were no complaints.

After a few years of unremitting hard work and solitude, Great-Grandpapa took a trip to Europe to find a wife. In due course, Mademoiselle Bachelier de St Marc, aged 17, was wooed and won, and they had a Hollywood-type midnight wedding in Bordeaux Cathedral, with a grand torchlight procession through the town, and much singing and feasting and rejoicing.

Great-Grandmamma, fresh from her convent, took to pioneering without turning a hair. The stabling of war-weary elephants in her garden could have been part of the nuns' training, so smoothly did she take such matters in her stride. Nocturnal visits from Chinese pirates sneaking up the river only prompted her to grope under her pillow in her sleep for her pistol, and having to turn her bungalow into an emergency hospital after one of the numerous local wars became a matter of routine. There is much to be said for the training of girls by nuns. Above all, they are realistic. The message which comes through, once you have worked your way past all the flummery, is clear and trenchant: 'Be adequate, and let nothing ruffle you.'

In due course, two sons were born to this gallant pair: Emile, a dreamy soul, who eventually sank his all in a mine tucked away in such an inaccessible part of the Borneo jungle that it has remained untouched to this day, and Leopold, my grandfather, who turned out to be a chip off the old block.

On Singapore Island Great-Grandpapa bought several

thousand more acres of land but, having cleared it of jungle, he then discovered that the soil was far less fertile than in Northern Malaya. To remedy this, and having noticed that the streets of Singapore were littered with uncollected refuse of every kind, he offered to clean up the town free of charge. The Governor, who hadn't got round to this ticklish problem himself, was only too glad to give his consent. So every day a procession of forty bullock-carts and five hundred men set out from Chasseriau Estate at the crack of dawn, and returned later with several tons of pungent but invaluable fertilizer, which was then ploughed into the land. And in no time at all, the plantation was the most prosperous on the island.

The crops included coffee, coconuts, sugar cane and tapioca, which was the favourite food of jungle pigs, who spent their nights rooting up the tasty tubers, thereby causing untold damage among the young trees. Great-Grandpapa's method of dealing with the problem was, against much opposition from the European and native population alike, to encourage visiting tigers to remain, settle down and breed on his land. And in their favour it must be said that they behaved like perfect guests, leaving the labour force intact and conscientiously gobbling up the pigs. The Comte de Jouffroy d'Abbans, who was French Consul at the time, and in whose memoirs I found these stories, relates that, on one of their walks through the plantation, when a tigress ambled nonchalantly past them with her young, my great-grandfather simply remarked, 'These are my cats. They do a good job. There's nothing like a few of them around to keep the mice down.'

D'Abbans's memoirs describe him as tall and broad-shouldered, a pioneer of the old type, indefatigable, sparing neither himself nor others, bellowing orders as he strode about among his men, demanding immediate and absolute obedience; but kind and just, and so never short of labour. Moreover, according to the Count, another reason why Great-Grandpapa, who employed over five thousand men, could always find as many as he wanted, was that he paid better wages than other employers. As most of his workmen were Muslims, he knew that their dearest wish was to get to Mecca, an expensive trip which they were able to afford after only a couple of years in his service. So as not to lose them when, as usual, they had squandered their return-passage money, and in order to enable them to get back, he posted an agent at the other end with instructions to lend funds to the improvident pilgrims, on condition that they worked off the loan at Chasseriau Estate on their return. (It was on this very plantation on Singapore Island that my father was interned by the Japanese when they overran Malaya almost a hundred years later.)

Once Chasseriau Estate was running smoothly, Great-Grandpapa decided to go back to France on leave. It was his last voyage. As they were approaching Aden, a violent storm blew up, washing a little girl overboard. Great-Grandpapa dived in after her, gashed his knee, and died of gangrene a few days later. According to the records, the authorities gave him 'an imposing funeral' in Aden where he is buried.

* * *

Meanwhile, at the other end of the world in Australia, Great-Grandfather Fesq moved with his family from one villa to another, according to the season or the mood of the moment. 'Lentana', particularly, according to Marie, was a scene of continual entertaining and lavish hospitality. Dinner parties, balls and concerts succeeded one another, and the afternoons were given over to those vast picnics to which the Victorians were so addicted.

When Marie joined the family, Papa's elder brother was 5 and his sister, my Aunt Mimi, was just born. Young Marie took to her like a duck to water, and they were inseparable for many years to come.

Uncle Bunny, Papa's elder brother, was an extrovert, a tomboy and always in trouble. He ran away from school and was locked up in the attic for several days with only bread and water. My father was totally different – shy and sensitive to a morbid degree. When it came to children's parties, he clawed at the railings, crying and begging to be left at home, and had to be wrenched away and carried to the party in tears. When he was 17, and the appalling prospect of dances and balls loomed, his legs most conveniently gave out and he became miraculously paralysed. Doctors and specialists were called in, and massage and mud baths were tried, all to no avail. Young Emile thankfully took to his crutches, hobbling about the house, feeling safe for life.

But he had reckoned without Marie's fierce determination. She formed her plan. Ordering the carriage one fine day, she took him and the housekeeper for a drive in the country.

When the chosen spot was reached, she told the coachman to stop, and they all climbed out for a little walk, my father hopping along quite cheerfully on his crutches, the three of them chatting amicably together. Reaching a grassy bank, they stopped for a rest. Without warning, Marie suddenly seized the crutches and flung them as far away as she could.

'And now', she said firmly, 'walk back, or stay here by yourself.' And grabbing the startled housekeeper by the arm, she marched her back to the carriage. I don't know how long it took young Emile to join them, or how he managed it, but he never used his crutches again.

Within a couple of years the spirit of adventure had taken possession of him, and he set sail for the East, quite literally standing on his own two feet. As far back as I can remember, until a couple of years before his death, he was the most indomitable walker I have ever known. When nearly eighty, on his visits to London he used to march me along the Embankment, over Chelsea Bridge, and back by Albert Bridge in twenty minutes flat. I panted after him with aching back and out of breath, but he was undaunted.

My father's search for adventure brought him to Malaya, where he met and married my mother in 1919. There are some splendid photographs of the wedding, taken under palm trees festooned with creepers hanging over the guests' heads like Christmas decorations. My father, for whom this must have been a terrible ordeal, worse than any of the balls in his teens, looks squashed, diminished, shrunken, half his usual size. I still cannot imagine how he went through with it, and can only put it down to Marie's early upbringing that he did not revert to crutches under the strain.

When I was born, an *amah* was found who seemed able to keep me, by some special magic of her own, as quiet as a fish throughout the day and night. Nobody had ever seen such a placid and contented baby. It was not until my parents were packing to come to Europe that the *amah*'s magic was discovered, tucked away behind my cot, in the shape of a bottle of chloroform. That was when Marie, who was still in Sydney, was sent for, and she arrived in France more or less at the same time as we did.

5

One fine day Rubio appeared without warning at Mas Mistral. He had been a houseman to Aunt Mimi, Papa's sister, who had a villa in Spain at San Sebastian. Whether he had run away or been sacked, and why he came to us, I never discovered. And I don't suppose my parents ever even asked. They simply welcomed him, gave him a room, and put him on the payroll. A Spanish Basque, self-willed and short-tempered, with bright red hair and bright red political views, Rubio had great natural elegance and bore himself like a grandee. He spoke a peculiar language of his own, probably a mixture of various kinds of patois, and he made sure we all picked it up as soon as possible, since he had no intention of learning any French.

From the start Rubio decided that his chief amusement would be baiting Marie, and he became the bane of her life. He would wait until she was ready to feed her hens, then creep up to the chicken-run, open the door and stand aside to let them out. At the same time he whistled through his teeth a special kind of hen-call which brought them running. Marie would come staggering up the path with her heavy buckets of food just in time to see her last Orpington vanish into the vineyard with a cheerful waggle of her tail-feathers. For the next hour or so we would try to help her round them up, leaping through the vines and whooping like Indians, while they scuttled back and forth, growing more and more hysterical, and sometimes taking to the air. It was a wild scene, with Marie flouncing around purple with rage, glasses flashing in the sun and hat flapping up and down like an eagle's wings. 'Catch them, you idiot,' she yelled, as I jumped about, as excited as the hens. And the long bamboo cane with which she conducted operations would come swishing down on the backs of my legs.

On two or three occasions, and I don't think Rubio could have been responsible for these, the hens went quite mad, started to pluck one another and laid eggs without shells, which they scattered all over their run in the most untidy way possible. Marie decreed that they needed calcium, bought a dozen oysters a day for the next fortnight and fed them the crushed shells, which meant of course that we had to eat the oysters. After trying one, which wriggled its way down my throat in the most horrible manner, I refused to touch another and left the rest for John and Anne, who thoroughly enjoyed the treat. The hens soon produced respectable shells again, and everything returned to normal.

Rubio decided that his chief job was to watch over us every moment of the day, and to act as my mother's bodyguard. Whenever she went out on her own, he followed, carrying her shopping, her umbrella, letters for posting, or whatever it happened to be. This drove her mad at first, but as he couldn't be shaken off, she came to accept it as inevitable. Marie, who refused to speak his own language, gave him orders in French, which he invariably disregarded. Their relationship never improved.

On the walk to church on Sunday, my father always with a newspaper ready under his arm to while away the time, Rubio brought up the rear, muttering fiercely all the way, and from time to time shaking his fist when his feelings got too much for him. As a confirmed Communist he strongly disapproved of these expeditions, but for nothing on earth would he have stayed behind and let us go on our own. As soon as we arrived, the curate, who was rather apprehensively looking out for us, would lead us firmly to a side-chapel where we were decently tucked away out of sight. You couldn't really blame the poor man, what with my father rustling *The Times*, Marie nodding and snoring, and Rubio cursing and shaking his fist as soon as the sermon started.

Once a year in spring, when the chimneys were swept and Madame Rose had to let her kitchen range go out, a cooking fire was built outside, between two large stones. Across these was placed a huge cauldron filled with sauerkraut and sausages, smoked pigs' cheeks, trotters and tails. Sitting on the grass around the fire, we all took part in the feast. The farmer came along, and the gardeners left their digging, spat on their hands and rubbed them together, then touched their caps and squatted by the fire. Caroline came croaking and hobbling over from her laundry troughs, her hands all white and wrinkled from years of soaking in cold water, and Pauvre Claire, with her forehead crinkled with worry and her mouth pursed up like a hen's bottom, handed out plates, glasses, knives and forks. We sat in silence, inhaling the delicious aroma wafting out of the pot, while a couple of bottles of Papa's wine stood 'breathing' in the grass. Then Madame Rose would dish up and we would all fall to.

Rubio never joined us in these feasts, whether by choice or because he was not invited I have no idea. But once at least he made sure we didn't get our treat. The home-made sauerkraut had as usual been scooped out of its barrel in the cellar, and all the various bits of smoked pork and sausages had been brought up to the house by the farmer the day before. The fire had been lit early in the morning, and Madame Rose had set her brimming pot over the blaze. But when she came back towards noon to dish up, she found it stone-cold. There was consternation all round. After an inquest, Rubio owned up to kicking the fire away from the pot soon after it was lit. There was an almighty row, and everyone turned on him with pungent oaths. But he just leaned back against an orange tree, smirking and picking his teeth with a pine needle.

When, years later, war broke out and we were all scattered across the world, Rubio stayed on at Mas Mistral while Marius moved into the old house, which he claimed as his own as soon as Mussolini entered the war and invaded the South of France. One day Rubio was found dead in the garden, where he probably still lies buried, since Marius would never have spent any money on a funeral for him.

* * *

As far back as I can remember, we longed for friends. Other children were a rare treat in our lives, and knowing they were regarded as a bad influence by Marie made them all the more desirable.

Our first attempt at friendship was with Clement, one of the flea-bitten brood belonging to the doomed farmer who brought our milk every evening. We did our best, but it was uphill work. Clement really didn't understand anything. We gave him marbles and lent him our rag dolls. We showed him how to get deliciously giddy by rolling down grass slopes. All to no avail. If he thought anything at all, it was probably that we were even more batty than his brothers and sisters. As his clothes were always falling off him in strips, we stole needles and thread from Pauvre Claire's sewing basket and tried to stitch him together.

'What are you doing?' he shouted, pulling away, as John stuck a large darning needle through his sleeves and right into his arm.

I sat on his legs to immobilize him. 'Can't you see you're falling to pieces? It won't take long. Do stop wriggling,' I implored.

'Get off me,' he yelled, flinging me away.

The friendship had no future. We had to abandon it.

Another promising relationship which also came to nothing, entirely through our own fault, was with a boy called Marc, whose parents brought him to tea one day. It was all to do with the zip-fastener on Marc's sweater, which was the first we had ever seen. While the grown-ups were conferring downstairs, we dragged him away to Papa's study for experimental purposes. There we held him down, while each in turn worked the zip up and down in great excitement. As a new invention, it was fascinating. But suddenly there was a fearful scream as a twitch of skin on his neck got caught in the zip. He leaped away and galloped downstairs, howling at the top of his voice. That night we went to bed without supper, and we never saw Marc again.

Next door to the house where D. H. Lawrence had recently died there lived a girl of about my own age called Marina, whose wisdom and knowledge of the world dazzled us and filled us with admiration. She told us the facts of life, and although we didn't believe a word she said, we were immensely impressed by her imagination and ingenuity in inventing such extraordinary tales. Mamma, who disliked Marina and probably thought her lewd and knowing, discouraged the friendship. She probably wanted to protect our innocence, but she need not have worried. As backward children, we were hard to beat. Although later, in Malaya, we became intimately acquainted with the mating habits of the snakes, mammals and insects all around us, the penny never dropped. These, we thought, were just more of their quaint and fascinating ways. We didn't get the message for a long time to come.

Marina's father was slowly dying of 'cancer of the heart'. Every morning after breakfast she would stump up the path and whistle for us to come and hear the latest news of the advancing disease. We were riveted by the gruesome details, and still more by her detached attitude towards the poor man's agony. We remembered with shivers of horror the time when Papa had stepped on a large nail which had gone right through his foot. So Marina's lack of feeling for her father's suffering was mystifying and confusing.

After a long-drawn-out agony which we shared with him through every stage until the death-rattle, he was gathered at last. A special doctor with a 'suitcase full of knives' came down from Paris to gut and embalm him, and pack him up for dispatch to Brazil where he was to be buried. And Marina told us with great pride that she had been allowed to have his heart, pickled in a bottle, beside her bed for the night before the departure of the corpse.

To our grief, Marina soon became too much for her mother to manage, and was packed off as a boarder to a convent in Nice. Years later I saw a photograph of her in a magazine, looking like a film-star in the Fascist uniform of the Italian army.

Another friend we lost, in tragic circumstances, was Gina, the postman's little daughter. Every winter, death and destruction, in one form or another, struck Vence and the surrounding villages. In those days children's diseases often turned into terrible epidemics, which spread alarmingly over wide areas. That year diphtheria raged in Vence, wiping out half the child population of the district. Our postman's daughter was among them, and the poor man was heartbroken. Trying to cheer him up, we offered him a glass of my father's wine, and led him to our favourite spot under the orange trees behind the kitchen.

As soon as Marie saw us, she came out with a bottle and a couple of glasses, and they both consoled each other as best they could. She had lost a son, and he a daughter. After that he would stop most days for a chat and a glass of wine. We all became great friends. Although they both detested *les Boches*, he and Marie thoroughly enjoyed a natter in German, as he came from Alsace and knew the language well. This was very boring for us, as we couldn't understand a word.

Seated on a kitchen chair opposite Marie, with the bottle between them, the postman would bring out the contents of the mailbag. Every time he fished out a postcard he read it out to us, so we were always kept abreast of local news.

'Ah ha!' he would say, pulling out a plum. 'This is for Madame Bichet, from her son who is doing his service in Algiers. He says his corporal is a pig. I bet he is!' or else, 'Mademoiselle Dupont has just got engaged, to Alfred Bejat of all people.' As we didn't know the young man in question, it meant nothing to us. But Marie would nod knowingly. And from time to time he would exclaim, 'Here is one for you, Madame Marie. From one of your step-daughters. You'd better read it yourself,' and hand it gallantly to her.

Marie's suspicion of 'other children' was confirmed when Anne, who was still quite small, nearly met her death at the hands of the local juvenile strangler. Polo, who was about 13 at the time and had the strength of a man, used to stalk the countryside looking for opportunities to practise his favourite hobby. And from time to time, on our walks through the woods, we would come across chickens with their heads pulled off, or the corpse of a lamb without any legs, and we knew that Polo had passed that way

On the day he had a go at Anne, she had wandered off down the path at the bottom of the garden. Knowing her ways, I expect she was pottering along, picking at the hedgerows and telling herself one of her interminable fairytales. Probably she didn't see Polo until he had pounced on her and got her by the throat. Her piercing yells brought help in the nick of time from a nearby peasant, and she got away with no more than a bad fright and a few bruises on her neck. But after that, whenever we sallied forth beyond our boundaries, we kept our eyes skinned for Polo, and ran for our lives if he ever appeared within a hundred yards.

My mother reported the incident to the Mayor, but nothing was done. A couple of years later Polo, by then a hefty teenager, was still striding around the countryside like Frankenstein. One day he burst into the village school and tried his luck in a classroom full of girls. This time the parents got up a formal petition which produced the desired result. Polo vanished from the scene. We never saw him again, and we often wondered what had happened to him. There wasn't much hope of treatment for psychopaths in those days, and the thought of poor Polo, the wild creature of the woods, cooped up in a cell with a ball and chain, haunted us for a long time.

* * *

From time to time Mamma took us to visit our neighbours, the Hilliers, who lived about half a mile away from Mas Mistral and were the only English people in the area. As a perfect example of the backbone of Old England, they stuck to tradition in everything they did, and even managed to create a real English garden in their patch of cracked, sun-baked clay. There were lawns, rockeries and herbaceous borders, and two of those heavenly cyprus trees which continually crop up in early Italian Renaissance paintings, with very smooth pale-grey trunks and close-packed foliage pointing up to the sky like minarets. It was a dream of a garden.

But the Hilliers were not entirely happy. Their Provençal *bonne-à-tout-faire* couldn't manage, try as she might, to produce traditional English puddings, fruit cake, Victoria sponges or first-class steak-and-kidney pie, so she was replaced by a man who had been a cook in the Royal Navy. All went well until the poor fellow, unhinged by loneliness, took first to the bottle and then to the hills, where he was found three days later raving under a juniper bush.

Throughout all these vicissitudes, Mrs H remained calm and unperturbed. She produced a baby, for which she made a cheerful chintzy nursery – so unlike our own, with its photographs of Marie's dead husband and baby glooming over us day and night. Then she got down to the Victoria sponges herself. I loved helping her in the kitchen, and I enjoyed looking after the baby when she was busy in the garden.

One fine summer afternoon, Mrs Hillier dropped in for tea. To our surprise, although we were playing quite noisily under the drawing-room window, we weren't called in to pay our respects. After an hour of earnest confabulation, she reappeared, and as we ran up to greet her, we heard her saying, 'So you see, my dear, we must stick together.'

'Of course,' my mother replied fervently. 'I quite agree with you.'

'If it weren't for the baby,' added Mrs H, 'I would go myself.'

'Don't worry,' said Mamma, 'I will go tomorrow, and the children will come with me.'

After our guest had left, we were informed of the treat in store. A family of Poor Whites had apparently settled in Vence and were squatting in utter penury in a deserted farmhouse at La Sine. It was generally believed that they came from Ireland, that the husband was an alcoholic, and that the numerous children who ran about barefoot were starving, since the family was totally destitute. Mrs H, having had wind of the affair, and not wanting to get mixed up in it herself, had tackled my mother, knowing she wouldn't be turned down.

And how right she was! Mamma, throwing herself into the venture full-tilt, made us bring her our rucksacks and filled them to the brim with all the preserves she could lay her hands on – home-made jam, pickled goose, chicken-liver pâtés, quails in brandy, and all kinds of preserved fruit out of the garden. Also the last pot of honey from our own bees, whose sacrifice I welcomed as good riddance.

Next morning, booted as if for mountaineering, we harnessed ourselves to our rucksacks, picked up an alpenstock each, and set off down the hill and across the valley to La Sine. Eventually we reached the clearing described by Mrs H. And there indeed stood the old farmhouse with its tiny windows like half-closed eyes, rather battered about the roof and top floor, but spacious enough to house a large family of Poor Whites. A huge chestnut tree spread its branches over the roof, and all around grew the finest, shortest emerald grass I had ever seen. It could have been a well cared-for bowling-green. Surrounding this fairytale spot were olive groves, cypresses and orange trees, and no other house in sight. But everywhere, right up to the front door, were piles of old tins and empty beer bottles and literally hundreds of wine bottles.

As we approached a dog barked and a pack of young children came pouring out of the house, followed by their mother. She stared at us in silence as Mamma explained the object of our visit. As we moved nearer the front door, the dog snarled and barred the way. We didn't appear to be welcome. The woman continued to glare at us without a word, and Mamma said, 'I expect the lady is busy. She wasn't expecting us. Unpack, children, and put your stuff on the grass.'

While we did as we were told, I took a quick look round at the children, a scruffy mob who were milling excitedly about, picking things up and running to their mother, screeching in some unknown language with vaguely English-sounding vowels. Monolithic and silent, the woman continued to stare, until the last pot stood on the ground. Then, in icy tones, she asked, 'And who do I owe this lot to?'

'I am a neighbour of Mrs Hillier's,' chirruped my mother.

'And these are my children. You are Mrs O'Connor, I presume?'

'Correct,' snapped the woman.

'What a lovely family you have,' prattled Mamma, lying through her teeth as the grubby-looking mob milled around noisily. At that moment a bulky, lumpy girl a couple of years older than me came out of the house. 'My step-daughter,' said Mrs O'Connor, mentioning no names. The girl stared in silence.

On the way home after this curiously unrewarding experience, relieved of our load, we skipped along merrily, picking wild flowers and peering into the bushes, looking for birds' nests. This was the end of the Poor Whites as far as we were concerned. But we still didn't know our mother.

'What a charming family,' she said, as I was extricating Anne from a bog into which she had sunk to her knees. 'We must have them round to tea, and you will look after the children, won't you?' she said, tapping me on the head with a hazel twig. My heart sank into my mountain boots, and all joy fizzled away.

When it came to the point, the small rabble, thank goodness, had been left behind, and all I had to deal with was the lumpy girl. John and Anne, needless to say, had vanished, so I took her upstairs to my room and introduced her to my favourite doll. The girl, whose name I still didn't know, stared in bored silence.

'Would you like to see my books?' I tried next. And then suddenly a thought struck me. 'You *can* read, can't you?' I asked tactlessly. She gave me a withering look, but there was no reply. 'Oh heavens,' I thought, 'now I've put my foot in it.' Completely at a loss about what to do with this unresponsive creature, I decided to take things in hand and ask no more questions. 'Come,' I said firmly, 'we'll walk round the garden.'

I showed her our animal cemetery, the goldfish in the pond, the strawberry beds, and the birds' nests in the hedge. By then we had almost reached the top of the garden. 'And here the donkeys from next door come through a hole in the fence to eat our raspberries.'

Further up was an anthill. 'If you step on it, the ants will chew your toes off,' I informed her.

A little way on we reached an adder's nest, heaving with black, wormlike babies. At the sight of them she sprang back as if she'd been bitten – but still didn't utter a word. By the time we got to the top of the garden, I was at my wits' end. This is my last effort, I thought. After that she can go to hell.

'This is my favourite tree. You can climb it if you like,' I said, offering the ultimate in hospitality. 'When you reach the top, you get a really good view of people dying in their beds on the terrace over there.' I pointed out the TB hospital where the poor patients, lying in the blazing sun, were coughing their lungs out, and giving up the ghost at the rate of two or three a day. Only then did it dawn on me that the girl couldn't understand a word I said because I was speaking French.

After that, I am glad to say, there were no more visitations from the Poor Whites.

6

Not long after this futile expedition my father suddenly and without explanation returned to Malaya, to Assam Java, the plantation he owned in Selangor. Since the reason for his departure was never discussed, we never knew whether he had always meant to go back, had lost money in the slump or was just plain bored with both us and the tame life of the South of France.

To us, it seemed like the end of the world. A feeling of doom settled on the house as the leather trunks were brought down from the attic, Papa's books were gathered from the shelves in the study, and Caroline gave his tropical gear a good bashing with the old cricket bat.

When the dreadful day arrived our grief was overwhelming. Blind with tears, we clung to Papa as he got into the taxi with Mamma, who was going to see him off from Marseilles. And although Marie took us all down to see the animals of a circus which had just arrived in the town, we went on snuffling for the rest of the day. Not even the antics of the king penguins could cheer us up, nor even the news that in a few months we too would be going to Malaya. At that stage a few months was like a hundred years.

Another twilight period of gloom and depression settled on

the house when Marie, who had never taken a holiday since she arrived in Vence, decided to go and visit her family in Switzerland before we left for the Far East. She would be deserting us for a whole month, while a niece of hers called Frieda took over. Passionately devoted to Marie as we were, her stand-in hadn't a chance.

A buxom blonde with a smooth face and eyes so wide apart they looked like headlamps, Frieda was probably a nice enough girl. And we might have found some of her habits rather quaint in a harmless sort of way, if we hadn't felt so abandoned and miserable. She made us eat on our own, whereas Marie always shared our meals. We had been trained, between courses, to keep our hands in our laps. But Frieda insisted we put them on the table, on either side of the plate. This, we thought, made us look like begging dogs, and lacked dignity. It was a small thing, but we felt it keenly, and when she took us for our first walk up the hill, we had our revenge. Without prearrangement of any kind, we all hurled our straw hats high up into a peach tree, from where there was no way of retrieving them. Frieda was furious. It was the beginning of a war that continued until Marie's return. From then on there were no more walks, and we, who were used to being out of doors all day long were confined to the nursery upstairs, 'doing time'.

No prisoner could have felt his confinement more acutely. Summer was just beginning, and we longed to be out of doors. The sun shone in a cloudless sky, and butterflies hovered thick and heavy over the wisteria on the balcony. Birds were in full song, and in the cherry tree outside our window maybugs buzzed, buzzed, buzzed incessantly. It was more than we could stand. So when Anne announced she wanted to go to the loo, we decided to take her to a downstairs one instead of the one on our own floor. Even an outing like this would be a treat after the oppressive dreariness of the nursery.

I don't know which of us tripped, but we all hurtled down head-first and crashed to the bottom, still holding hands. Frieda burst out of the kitchen, smacked us all soundly and drove us back to the nursery. From then on we were *locked* in. As caged animals often do, we stopped eating, wilted and sickened. It was probably no more than a summer cold, but the full treatment went into operation at once. And this cure was far worse than the passing misery of a sniffle and a cough.

Home treatment for minor ailments was the bane of childhood in those days. Castor oil was a constant terror, dished out at regular intervals, whether needed or not. Bags of scalding porridge were clamped to the chest for coughs, after which, if the cough developed into wheezing tubes, came 'cupping'. A piece of cotton wool was lit inside a glass to create a vacuum and this was clamped to the skin of the back, which immediately began to swell and turn bright purple. You were lucky when it was left at that. For pneumonia the glass was wrenched off and a cross slashed into the spongy, swollen skin. Blood gushed, letting out the infection, and all symptoms were expected to vanish overnight. We never had to suffer this particular form of torture ourselves. But when John had his tonsils out, the operation took place at home. Marie held him between her knees, his jaws were jacked apart with a clamp, and our local doctor carried out the job as best he could in the night nursery.

When my mother and I returned from the chicken-run to which we had fled from the sound of John's terrible screams, he was lying on his bed in a swoon. Marie, impassive as a Henry Moore statue beside him, was mopping up the blood which oozed from his swollen mouth. And the tonsils and adenoids were floating in a jam-jar on the table beside her.

We were only just back on our feet, recovering from our treatment, when Marie returned from her holiday in Switzerland. Ecstatic with relief and happiness, we waited for her all morning at the garden gate. And when the railway cart finally appeared, with her sitting next to the coachman, we skipped along beside them all the way up to the house. As soon as they stopped at the dining-room door, we flew into her skirts with whoops of joy, delivered at last from our month of purgatory. The shabby railway cart was a chariot of gold, while the old nag which pulled it was Pegasus in all his glory!

* * *

I never discovered why we didn't all travel to Malaya together. Perhaps Papa couldn't face the thought of being cooped up in a boat with his family for three whole weeks. Whatever the reason, a few months after his departure we travelled to Marseilles and took ship aboard the *Insulinda*, a gallant long-distance liner sailing under the Dutch flag. I was going back to the land of my birth, and John and Anne were visiting it for the first, though not the last, time in their lives.

Marie and the three of us were packed into a cabin as small and cosy as a squirrel's nest, where she managed somehow to stow everything away with a minimum of grumbling. There was nothing she loved so much as a good long voyage, rough seas and plenty of storms. She had even been lucky enough to be shipwrecked on one occasion, with the boat splitting asunder and the two halves drifting away in opposite directions. She may well have been hoping for some dire calamity to overtake us on this voyage, but disappointingly nothing really exciting happened, apart from a few heavy storms.

Mamma presumably had a cabin to herself, but where it was and what it was like we never discovered, as we were never invited to visit her during the voyage. We hardly ever saw her, except occasionally playing quoits on an upper deck or sometimes lying in a canvas chair with a book. Adults and children occupied different decks, and we had our meals in our very own children's dining-room.

Every corner of the *Insulinda* reeked of the most divine smells of tar, wood, oil and all the peculiar emanations which always waft out of a ship's hold. To this was added the sharp tang of the sea, all of which combined in such a potent mixture that every time I have come across it since, the memory of that first voyage comes back with compelling vividness. And though we were almost a month at sea, I don't remember a moment of boredom.

Before the novelty had worn off we were at Port Said,

where we stopped to take on fuel for the engines. Thousands of sacks of coal came on board on the backs of an endless procession of men who looked, from the upper deck, like a double line of ants, one coming up the gangway, the other flowing in the opposite direction. For several days after that an overpowering smell of coal hung about, and everything was covered with black dust, as not the faintest breeze blew while we crept through the Suez Canal, preceded by a ponderous dredger. Once we saw a mirage, a sheet of shimmering water hanging in the sky, with camels ambling slowly below.

It was a relief to be out in the open sea again and to feel the live water whipping the sides of the ship. But the Red Sea didn't live up to its name. This was disappointing, as we were looking forward to cruising over an enormous expanse of blood-coloured water, with bright-red waves crashing right up to the deck.

As we nosed our way into the Indian Ocean the weather grew warmer, and the steward stripped a couple of blankets off our bunks, then showed us how to open the porthole. 'You must always shut it during storm,' he said in his heavy Dutch accent, 'or you will be drowned in your slip if the sea come in.'

He got on well with Marie. They gossiped in German, and he brought us innumerable bottles of mineral water, as we were forever thirsty – all that salt in the air, and of course you couldn't drink the tap water. He filled our baths to the brim (a luxury never allowed at home), saying there was plenty more where that came from, and the fish wouldn't miss it. He hung about with huge towels, and I think he would even have scrubbed our backs if Marie had allowed it. On his afternoons off he joined us in a game of lotto, and spoke of his little girl in Holland, saying how much he missed her. He was a kind man, and we invited him to come and live with us in Selangor. Rubio had been left behind at Mas Mistral, and we felt we could do with a man about the place again. But he declined, on account of his little girl.

In the Indian Ocean we saw our first whale, spouting high in the air. Schools of dolphins followed us for days, and flying fish swam alongside, skimming through the spray at great speed. We all seemed to be travelling in the same direction.

Then the sharks appeared.

An Indian *ayah* had died on board, and was brought up to our deck, sewn into a sack. We all stood in a circle while the padre read the funeral service, after which a plank was placed on the rail, her body was laid on it, and it slid straight into the midst of the cruising sharks.

These creatures, Marie told us, had a fiercely tenacious hold on life. On one of her voyages to or from Australia, a sailor had harpooned one and hauled it up on deck. He cut out the shark's heart, which went on beating for five hours, long after its body was thrown back into the sea.

Marie was convinced that sharks had supernatural powers. She had seen a man paddling in Botany Bay in a few inches of water, where he thought he was safe. Little did he know that a shark, having become invisible through its own magic, had sneaked up close to him for a quick bite. Suddenly the poor man found himself planted in the sand on his ankle stumps, with both his feet neatly clipped away from under him.

The *Insulinda*, being a small ship, pitched and rolled a good deal. In the Indian Ocean we encountered several storms, and since nearly all the passengers were laid low and we were never sea-sick, we had the entire boat to ourselves. Marie would take us up on deck, where we were soon drenched by the monsoon rain and the enormous waves which crashed over us. As lightning flashed across the sky, and thunder roared and rumbled all around, she told us that it was in a storm such as this that she had experienced her first shipwreck.

After a good soaking-through on deck, she would take us down to the saloon, where she bullied the barman into brewing us a strong reviving pot of tea. This was produced under protest, in minute cups, and there was a battle every time over getting a refill. Deprived of her sustaining feuds with Rubio, Marie was always on the lookout for another sparring partner. Most men were terrified of her, but the Dutch barman enjoyed the fights as much as she did, and stood his ground.

After tea we would return to our cabin and help Marie put her feet up, tucking them into shawls and pillows to ease her varicose veins. Twisted and lumpy, they stood out on her legs like an intricate network of old ivy climbing up a tree. There had apparently been an occasion when one of the veins had exploded, the blood 'shooting straight up in the air like a geyser'. This had been before our time, but we were taking no chances, and always made sure that Marie got her daily rest.

One of the decks had been roped off for children in such a

way that we were literally inside a cage of netting, up which we climbed, hanging giddily over the water when the boat pitched that way. As our companions were nearly all Dutch, we had to pick up some of their language in order to play with them. Unused as we were to other children, this daily contact completely went to our heads. We threw ourselves wildly at the swings, rocking horses, toy cars and engines, refused to give them up, and had to be dragged away kicking and screaming.

I was completely out of hand, and John and Anne, though more restrained, joined me at meals in catapulting peas with our forks across the table at our equally wild friends. Marie declared she had never seen us behave so badly. The influence of 'other children' was disastrous, and she longed for the end of the voyage, when she would have us to herself again, under control, and well away from the little Dutch terrors. We knew this state of affairs would not last for ever and that retribution would follow. So we made the most of it.

When it came to the turn of our elders to fool around and make an exhibition of themselves, however, we considered their behaviour quite grotesque and severely disapproved. The ceremony of 'Crossing the Line' when we reached the Equator seemed to us the most fatuous performance imaginable, as we watched the adults career around the deck in improbable fancy dress, screaming as buckets of sea-water were emptied over their heads. As the day went on they got noisier and more rumbustious, and we looked on in silent disapproval. We were glad to see that Mamma did not take part in these orgies, although we noticed with distaste, in our odious priggish way, that she laughed a good deal at them.

At last, after days and nights with nothing but sea and sky, we spotted a smudge on the horizon. The sight of it threw us into a state of wild excitement. Marie, instead of quelling us as she usually did, gave us a smile that was a clear sign of approval. And so, hardly knowing why, we whooped and leaped about the deck, yelling 'Land, land,' while she, tense and silent, gripped the rail and stared at the island of Ceylon in the distance. Who knows what adventures she was hoping for?

The harbour, when we eventually steamed up to the jetty, was full of canoes with small boys standing up in them, shouting and waving their arms. When someone threw a coin, they all dived in, and there was a tremendous scuffle under the surface, until finally one of them would come up with the coin in his teeth. Among them was a small boy with only one arm, and Marie told us the other one had been chewed off by a shark.

To our joy we were allowed a whole day off the ship. This was our first experience of a tropical island, and it fully came up to our expectations. The white deserted beaches and the waving palm trees, as soon as we got out of town, were pure Robinson Crusoe. The rickshaw man who jogged us around seemed to know exactly what we wanted to see. At noon we arrived at a small Chinese store made out of flattened petrol cans (this rather clashed with the Crusoe theme) and gorged ourselves on bananas, and a revolting kind of biscuit that tasted like castor oil – the only disappointment in an otherwise perfect day.

When we finally arrived in Singapore, Papa was on the quay to meet us. Our excitement at seeing him again was tempered by a sudden, unexpected fit of shyness. We had never seen him in tropical gear before. He looked odd and unfamiliar in his shorts and white topee. We were dazed by the noise and bustle of the harbour, and our legs felt like boiled cucumbers after our long weeks at sea. Our first encounter with the powerful smells of the East made us feel giddy, and it was a relief to get into a large and comfortable car.

Breakfast at Raffles Hotel brought yet another surprise. Cutting open what we thought was a luscious cantaloupe melon, we were faced with the little black seeds of the papaya. This was to become my favourite fruit. And there was plenty of it, as it grew like a weed in the garden of Assam Java.

In the afternoon we boarded another boat bound for Port Swettenham. I think at this point I must have fallen asleep, for I remember nothing more until we were climbing into Papa's old Fiat for the final stage of the journey, through the jungle, in the dark.

7

It was several days before a procession of bullock-carts came rumbling up the drive with our belongings, which were packed into several large wooden crates. It took Marie a good deal of grunting and grumbling to sort them all out, and find suitable corners and cupboards for our clothes and toys.

Although Assam Java was quite a large bungalow, there were few rooms as such, since most of its living space had been set out in an early form of open plan. The ground floor, which was built of concrete for coolness, was surrounded on three sides by trellises, over which climbed moonflowers, orchids and fire-cracker vines. Behind the house a covered way led to the kitchen and the servants' quarters.

A dozen or so stone pillars supported the first and only other floor, which held our bedrooms and the sitting-room, and was reached by a rickety wooden staircase steeped in creosote. When going to bed after supper, in the dark, we kept as far away as we could from the hand-rail, as Marie told us that was the way snakes usually got up to the first floor. The thought of laying your hand on the back of a python making for the bedrooms in search of a feast was spine-chilling.

We were never allowed to run, even barefoot, on this floor. No one knew exactly how strong the timbers were, or how far in the termites with which they were riddled had wormed their way. Our cousins in Kedah had jumped through their bathroom floor, landing on the concrete below, children, keeper, bathtub and all, and had sustained fearful injuries. After we left, Assam Java did in fact collapse like a pack of cards, but mercifully no one was in it at the time.

The first floor was surrounded by a large veranda and a mosquito screen, only ever used *after* we had gone down with malaria. There were no outside walls, but a few blinds, rotted to shreds by the sun and hanging askew on their strings, flapped around until one by one they were carried away by the wind. A thick curtain of plants enveloped the house, providing a leg-up for an unending stream of visiting lizards and insects. The landing walls were decorated with krises, kukris and all kinds of oriental swords collected by my father over the years. There were also various snake skins, some of which, cured by local craftsmen, were faded and crumbling. Others, treated in India by experts, shone and gleamed like polished silver.

On the right-hand side of the first-floor landing were our parents' bedrooms, bathroom and breakfast-room. Marie and the three of us children lived across the landing, on the opposite side. The night nursery was built of rough-hewn planks, soaked through with creosote in the vain hope of discouraging termites. There were no ceilings anywhere. We slept under the rafters and palm-leaf thatch, through which wriggled centipedes, lizards and all kinds of insects. An abundant fauna was born, lived and died above our heads. Rats and squirrels peered down at us, various creatures squeezed in and out of the palm-thatch and frequently crashed to the floor with a thud and a squelch. I once found a black and yellow snake curled up between my sheets. One morning his identical twin was nestling in my sandal. I don't know why we were never bitten.

As nobody seemed to worry, we took this constant shower of snakes and scorpions, centipedes and spiders in our stride. Most of them were tossed out of the window. But when a new creature unknown to us landed, Marie picked it up and dropped it into a jar of surgical spirits which she added to her collection of pickled snakes and other creatures on the night-nursery shelves. The handsome array of vivid greens, yellows and reds, sealed in by the spirits, was gay as a rainbow and never faded.

The top shelf of our night-nursery wall was occupied by a row of jam-jars filled with various breeds of scorpion with deadly stings, foot-long poisonous centipedes as fat as sausages, and several kinds of tarantula and bird-eating spiders. These amiable creatures – all very much alive – were fed on grilled insects from the dining-room table twice a day. A huge acetylene lamp hung, roaring like a motorboat, from a rafter and every airborne insect within a mile hurtled into it and dropped sizzling on to the tablecloth, cooked to a turn for our menagerie upstairs. A sheet of Bronco, stuck with air holes and held down with a rubber band, covered the jars. And wondrous to relate, none of the menagerie ever escaped.

The day nursery was open on all sides to anyone who

wished to enter. Miniature owls made free use of the opportunity and raised their families on top of the wardrobe. A small ladder was used by Titi, John's tame hen, for climbing into our clothes cupboard where she laid her eggs. We had found her as a very small chick, lying on her side with a broken leg, cheeping pathetically, unable to run after her mother. Clucking over her like a mother hen himself, John had gathered her up and carried her to the nursery, where Marie put the leg in a splint made of cotton wool and matchsticks: so expertly did she do it that Titi never had the slightest limp.

From then on we were her family. We fed her on a diet of hard-boiled eggs, bread soaked in Carnation milk, squashed flies and minced worms. Marie said the proper way of preparing worms for her was for us to chew them up first, and I actually saw her put this method into practice herself when dealing with a baby owl who was being difficult about his food. But our devotion never quite reached that level.

The nursery door, which looked as if it was made of ships' timbers, was fitted with a huge pig-iron lock and an assortment of rusty bars. The keys, as large as fire-irons, hung on a nail by the door, and were only ever used by the houseboys as weapons in their fights. The enormous keyhole made a cosy nesting box for lizards, which laid their tiny eggs inside. These we scooped out with a teaspoon and stored away in matchboxes. Within a few days the babies hatched, wriggling fiercely to get out. Try as we might, we never managed to tame them, and they departed ungratefully as soon as they had learned to open their matchboxes.

* * *

The entire household would usually be woken by Papa at 5 a.m. as he greeted the dawn with trumpetings of hay fever. He suffered from it all the year round, as John and I did. Soon after that, a houseboy brought our breakfast up to the day nursery. There were papayas, *pamplemousses*, passion-fruit and a special kind of mini-banana with such a powerful smell that a clump ripening in the garden would send all the monkeys mad for miles around. Sometimes, as a special treat, there were lengths of dripping sugar cane, but this wasn't grown in the garden as it attracted elephants. The butter, which came out of a tin, soaked like oil into the toast and needed a lot of jam to kill the taste. The stiff, syrupy milk, which also came out of a tin, is the only kind I have ever been able to swallow. We each had our own crate, and were allowed as much of it as we liked.

After breakfast came the morning walk. This followed a set pattern. We plunged straight into the plantation which surrounded the garden. Marie cruised ahead, large hat securely fastened and skirts billowing, a jam-jar in one hand and a forked stick in the other, her good eye scanning the undergrowth for any poisonous creature that might be lurking. From time to time she glanced at the creeper-covered trees above for a possible python. Whenever she sighted one, she drew out her whistle and blew a few sharp blasts. Instantly Tamils would appear from behind every tree. Their excitement, always on the boil, grew as they prepared for the capture. Shoving, pushing and shouting, they created an uproar that was echoed and magnified by the monkeys all around.

The capture would take a long time. Eventually a stout pole was cut and trimmed, and a length of wire with a noose at the end produced and raised in front of the snake. Its head danced about for a few minutes, and then suddenly it lunged forward and plunged straight into the trap. Hauling it down was a slow business. A few brave men climbed the tree to prise the tail loose, while those on the ground tied a rag around its jaws as soon as its head was within reach. From then on it was restrained and thrashed less fiercely. The great coils, loosening and sagging, were tied to a pole with wire and carried back to the bungalow.

The household was summoned to admire and exclaim over the capture and the bravery of the victors. There must have been a price on the head of every snake on the estate, for as soon as one was caught, Chinese tradesmen appeared and started bargaining for the entrails before the creature was even dead. We left them to it and resumed our walk. Marie, her hunter's instinct thoroughly roused by success, would march on ahead, followed by Anne and myself, each holding a paw of our tame household monkey.

We had found this little creature on one of our walks, abandoned at the foot of a tree, and she had become our most devoted pet. Her official home was a small box at the top of a long pole behind the bungalow, but she spent most of her time in the house, preferably sitting on your lap, or with her arms tightly clasped around your neck, breathing into your ear. But out in the jungle she cringed with fear at the screams and jeers of her wild relations leaping overhead.

Last in line came John, pushing my little doll's pram in which nestled Titi, tucked up to the chin, with her head on the pillow.

When we finally got back from our walk, we knew what to expect. The entire staff would be gathered around the snake in the garden. Looking out of the nursery window, we would see them milling around a huge tree-trunk lying on the ground and, stretched out down its entire length and nailed to it at both ends, the python being sliced open from head to tail. When the gut was extracted, one of the men would coil it up like rope and stuff it into a bag. This would eventually end up in Chinese chemists' shops as an expensive aphrodisiac. The workmen would get a good price for their catch. I was always horribly sick at these scenes.

Our daily 'jungle walks' usually lasted two or three hours, according to the heat, the luck of the day or Marie's mood. When we eventually got back, hot and tired, around eleven, we would be heartily greeted by 'the pack', led by Woo, the family chow. The rest of his gang, a scruffy lot he collected on his rounds, kept in the background, knowing their place. They were constant casualties of the hazards of life, and Woo had to replace them at frequent intervals. They were bitten by snakes, as they would never leave well alone, they gobbled up poisonous spiders, and sometimes I suspect they were kidnapped and ended up in a curry. In the end, only Woo was left. He had finally given up collecting strays, as he was getting too old to control them. His moods grew uncertain, and my mother, with the dread of rabies always uppermost in her mind, decided to find him another home. Poor Woo was given to a family friend in Kuala Lumpur, and we were heartbroken when we heard the news. But two days later, to our joy, Woo was back, wagging his tail, telling us what a clever dog he was to have found his way through fifty miles of jungle on his own.

* * *

The ground floor of the house, where we sat on cane chairs around a large bamboo table for our elevenses of fresh lime juice, papaya, mangostine, passion-fruit, giant grapefruit and whatever else might be in season, was dotted with straw-lined boxes. Here an assortment of creatures were tamed or trained, according to their needs, and the invalids, with broken wings or limbs, mended as best as we could with home-made splints. Baby birds fallen from the nest were wrapped in separate bundles and had to be fed several times a day with revolting wodges of mashed-up worms. These were stuffed straight into gaping craws with Marie's stamp-collecting tweezers. A little mongoose jumped up and down in a perpetual state of excitement, while the small grey monkey, who curled up on the first convenient lap, snatched any food she could get hold of.

Our stork usually joined us for elevenses. He had been

found hobbling along a jungle track with a broken wing, and was brought home by my parents in the middle of the night. He protested vociferously all the time his wing was in a splint, and went on objecting to everything forever after, even when his wing had healed and he was free to go whenever he chose. But in spite of hating us all, he stayed on and joined the family. Twice a day, down by the pond, Marie threw him fish, and he caught them in mid-air, which prowess he loved to show off by joining a side on the badminton court when my parents were enjoying a game on the lawn after tea, and catching the shuttlecock as it came flying over the net. At dusk he would fly to the top of the house where he roosted, squawking intermittently throughout the night.

Behind the bungalow was the hen-run, which was wired all over against hawks and other predators. But in spite of this, a ten-foot python, which had managed to squeeze through a hole in the netting, was found one morning trapped inside, unable to get out. There were four large lumps down the length of its body, where the hens it had gobbled had come to rest inside it, and these were now the cause of its undoing. Headed by Cooky waving a hatchet over his head, the house staff came running out of the kitchen whooping with glee. And that night there was a sumptuous feast in their quarters, so much more tasty than their usual bully-beef rations.

But quite apart from the unexpected snake invasions, the hen-run was never quiet. Its inmates were far more exotic than Marie's previous flock at Mas Mistral. Besides the usual hens there were ducks, geese, guinea-fowl, peahens and golden pheasant. But most deafening of all were the jungle fowl. In the morning they flew down from the rubber trees to join their friends in the hen-run. Unable to get in, they crowded at the door, screeching their heads off, so that everybody knew the jungle set had arrived for the day. Once inside, gobbling up the chicken food, they fiercely stood up to anyone who tried to get rid of them. In the evening all the fuss went into reverse, and they clamoured to be let out, growing more hysterical as night approached. As soon as the door was opened, up they flew in a great flurry back into the rubber trees where they presumably felt quite safe.

* * *

Cooky, who produced all our meals, was a Tamil of uncertain age. Always cheerful, whatever the situation, he had a vast paunch and a jolly countenance. His kitchen was a dark tin hut completely filled with smoke, and there were usually half a dozen men and boys crouching on the floor, blowing on the charcoal braziers. Except for a short and blissful period when a Chinese cook took over and spoilt us outrageously by producing a different menu every day of the week, we had Cooky's curries (mutton or hard-boiled eggs) day after day all the time we were at Assam Java.

The Chinese interlude unfortunately did not last very long. One day soon after his arrival, the new cook gathered the entire staff in the backyard, and the youngest houseboy came to collect us from the coffee trees where we were lurking at the time. He put a finger across his lips for silence and led us to the kitchen yard, where all the staff were standing in a circle around the new cook, who held a chicken in one hand and a chopper in the other. He sliced off the bird's head, then put it down on the ground. There was a rousing cheer from the whole company as the poor creature staggered forward a few feet, then collapsed in a pool of blood. At this point my mother swooped into our midst and drove us away, spitting out a few vitriolic words in Malay over her shoulder. And that was the end of a wonderful cook. Next day fat old Cooky was back on the job with his two menus.

Behind the kitchen along a covered passage were rows of white cells, which were the houseboys' bedrooms. A whole settlement of huts and thatched cabins housed the innumerable dependants of the indoor and outdoor staff. It was a constantly changing population, all fed and housed by Papa. Nobody knew or worried how many were in residence at any one time. New babies appeared and old people died. We often came across their funerals on our walks, and a jollier sight you never did see. The corpse, painted red all over, would lie on a litter decorated with flowers and carried shoulder-high by members of the family, who sang and laughed and jangled bells all the way. A good funeral was a hearty spectacle which set you up for the rest of the day.

Apart from the houseboys, who were always changing because of their quarrels and their fights, the *tottegaran*, or gardener, pottered about the garden, squatting in front of a plant here, contemplating a new papaya shoot there, but I never saw him do any actual *work*. He watched the bananas ripen, shooed away the monkeys, picked the mangoes before they dropped to a squelch on the hard earth below, brought the luscious passion-fruit to the pantry, and somehow wriggled in among the spiky leaves to cut the pineapples at the right moment. And perhaps after all that *was* his work.

Our postman (each estate had its own) was a bicycle expert. When my parents were at the Club, or in Kuala Lumpur, he would give us magnificent demonstrations of all the tricks he could perform on his machine – standing on the saddle with one foot on the handlebars, or standing on the pedals on his hands, or sitting backwards on the saddle, pedalling furiously forward. As likely as not, all this would take place on his return from the village, when the bicycle was fully loaded with the mail, and mutton rations from the Selangor stores. Since the job of postman occupied only two or three hours of his day, he had plenty of time for bicycle practice, and probably made a little extra on the side by giving performances at fairs and in the bazaars.

The *tanigaran* was the water wizard. Out of a putrid pond he produced drinkable water and filled the baths every day, and so carefully did he ration the monsoon rain that there was enough for hair-washing all year round. He wore his own hair in a little bun high up on the back of his head – as an outdoor man he didn't wear a turban, but his sarong was always clean and his beard neatly combed. He also did a turn every day at the 'laundry', standing beside the washing slab, trickling water from an old bucket on to the clothes which the *dhobi* whacked with another stone. In this manner, silk shirts and crêpe-de-chine nightdresses were mashed to a pulp in quite a short time.

Sandenam, the chauffeur, was a very superior person. Immaculately dressed in tussore jacket and calico sarong, he wore his hair smooth and short like a European. He had his own quarters behind the garage, where his wives and children led a jolly and colourful existence full of song and laughter. His smile, which came frequently, was a dazzling flash of gold, as his savings all went into his teeth. The best way to avoid robbery, he used to say, was to carry your fortune in your head. So whenever he had a few dollars to spare, off he went to his Chinese dentist in Kuala Lumpur to have another gold tooth drilled into his jaw.

He was a very good driver, and understood the car well, never taking it through more flood water than it could manage. With one exception, we never broke down in the jungle – an experience best avoided. When it did happen, our guardian angels must have been working overtime. We were free-wheeling downhill on our way back from a holiday in the mountains, screeching round hairpin bends, with the mountain on one side and on the other a sheer drop of several hundred feet into the jungle below. All at once the car dipped forward and we saw one of our wheels gaily bowling down the road ahead of us, making straight for the precipice. As we had no spare on board, we might have been stuck there all night, a welcome feast for the tigers, leopards and mountain bears of the area. There was very little traffic on that mountain road.

So it was with bated breath that we watched our wheel approaching the edge.

Suddenly, out of nowhere, a low stone wall a few feet long appeared beside the road. As if guided by an invisible hand, the wheel came to rest gently against that wall. At the same moment, a lorry came chugging round the bend, and the Malay driver, seeing our problem, stopped and came over to help. He had the tools that Sandenam had forgotten to pack, so the wheel was on again in no time. But my mother would not let us watch the operation and led us away down the road until the job was done. It appeared the lorry-driver was a leper. His nose and top lip were missing, which gave him the fearsome look of a live and grinning skull. At this point I realized that Mamma's ban on jungle stops might well be justified.

* * *

Unlike my grandfather, who rode or drove a carriage wherever he went, Papa walked everywhere. After a cup of tea, he would set off on his rounds of the plantation, the factory, the drainage and the villages. On and on he trudged with only a stick to ward off cobras, for seven or eight hours on end, checking, examining, inspecting everything. At two o'clock he was back for lunch, and after a couple of hours' rest he would go into his office to stir up the sleeping clerks, who snoozed the day away with their feet on their typewriters.

Once a week, the workmen filed past the office window to be handed their pay-packet and rice ration. The queue was long and slow-moving, as Papa had a word with each man or woman as he gave them their wages.

Punishment for wrong-doing was dispensed on home ground in those days. Minor and major offences (anything up to murder) had to be dealt with on the spot and Father was, perforce, judge and executioner. So many strokes of the rattan, according to the offence, were administered on the lawn outside the office. And watching these thrashings from the nursery window, I remember how much more sorry we felt for Papa than for the victim. Sensitive, fastidious and withdrawn as he was, this part of his job was an ordeal. But there was no shirking it if he wanted to keep the respect of his men. The *tuan* had to do his duty, like everybody else. His reputation as a just and good man survived the war, so that afterwards, when he was released from internment, he was allowed to walk everywhere, unarmed and unmolested, in a bandit-infested country.

* * *

Roaming the garden was, for us, the next best thing to jungle walks. We happily spent entire mornings watching the traffic around an ant's nest, or crawling along a hedge hunting caterpillars by scent, as a dog follows a badger's trail. For hours on end we watched the humming-birds in all their dazzling colours, dead still apart from the blur of their wings, 'standing' in mid-air in front of a flower. Birds of every kind fluttered around, large and small, bright and dull, whistling, squawking, screeching. Moths and butterflies hovered like helicopters in the undergrowth, and giant dragonflies scythed through the air in crazy zigzags.

The antics of the monkeys were an endless source of fascination. Continually flying from tree to tree with shrieks and howls, they would stop from time to time to nibble a twig, peel a banana, have a good scratch, or pee over our heads. Then suddenly, for no particular reason, a furious uproar would break out and a glorious battle would follow. The audience cheered the fighters with hysterical whoops and wild leaps through the trees. Sometimes a baby lost its grip and dropped to the ground. And you had to pretend you hadn't noticed. As soon as you were safely out of the way, the mother would come down, grab the quaking infant, shake it to a jelly, and take it up into the trees again.

The coffee trees came into their own at blossom time. Shoulder to shoulder, so to speak, with the humming-birds, which came streaking across the garden from the hibiscus hedges where they normally lived, we hung around the flowers, breathing in the powerful smell, sneezing incessantly but unable to tear ourselves away. It was quite literally a drug, of which we could never have enough.

The humming-birds obviously felt the same way, as they remained until the last coffee flower shrivelled and died, when we all returned to our habitual occupations. The coffee seeds would then appear, and very soon turn bright red, when we helped Cooky to pick them. They were roasted in the back yard, and I am sure that there is no more divine smell in the world than freshly picked coffee roasting in the open air.

On the right side of the house was the mud-filled pond round which the stork hopefully paddled all day long in search of fish. But all it contained was a stinking mess of decayed leaves that had fallen off the rubber trees into the only water supply available for drinking, baths and laundry.

This was made fit for use in a miraculous way through my mother's ingenuity. Several huge, porous earthenware jars, which stood in a row beneath the house on wooden stands, were always kept filled to the brim with the slimy liquid. Brought in straight from the reeking pond, it was poured into the first jar, thick, brown and stinking of rotten rubber. All day and all night it oozed through the earthenware, filtering away, drip-drip into a bucket underneath. When this was full, its contents were poured into a second container from which the liquid trickled down into its own pail. And so on all the way down the line, until it reached the last jar. By the time it had worked its way through to this stage, it was as clear as rainwater. My mother then added a few crystals of potassium permanganate, and the job was done. The resulting brew was mixed with fresh lime juice for our breakfast, and my parents added whisky to theirs.

Our daily bath, after the siesta, was another problem. The *tanigaran* brought us buckets of the pond's untreated contents, in which we had to soak. No amount of carbolic soap could kill the smell or dissolve the thick brown slime on our skin. Peeling it off with a towel was excruciating agony. We begged to be let off this daily torture, pointing out that we always came out more dirty and smelly than before we went in. But no amount of pleading did any good.

* * *

There were times when a fearful commotion suddenly broke out among the workmen in the garden. The headman would come pelting across the lawn, shouting that one more Tamil had been eaten by a crocodile while drawing water from the river. Among the three or four of these monsters that patrolled our stretch of the stream there was one legendary brute, so old and gnarled and battered that he looked like a rotting tree-trunk as he lay in wait by the river bank. We often saw him there, snoozing in the mud with his tail hanging in the water, on our morning walks. He was a wily old rogue, and the workmen, who should have known better, walked straight into his jaws every time. It was a matter of constant amazement to us that anyone, especially those as experienced as our workmen, could so easily be taken in by the decrepit old devil. On each occasion my father lectured the whole village at great length on the lawn, where they stood wailing and lamenting their loss. They could not believe they were in any way to blame.

Every time, a goat was attached to a hook which hung from the tree under which the croc lay in wait for his prey. Many of these poor creatures were sacrificed in the hope of catching the old brute. But he always managed to pick off the goat and dodge the hook. Then suddenly one morning, soon after the end of the monsoon, the clamour in the garden announced victory instead of the usual disaster. In his dotage, the battered old monster had at last lost enough of his cunning to fall into the trap. The workmen had dragged him up to the garden, and there he sprawled, limp and dead, looking infinitely obscene. The stench from his carcass was overpowering. Somebody propped his jaws open with a stick. There was one green tooth left among the folds of yellow fat which hung about loosely all the way down to his gizzard. It was reckoned he was at least a hundred years old.

When he was gutted, small bags of coins and a collection of bangles, earrings and various other trinkets were found in his vitals. That night there were great rejoicings in the Tamil villages. The tom-toms beat a triumphant tattoo until sunrise.

8

The tiny eggs used by Cooky for his curries were collected by the houseboys from the jungle fowls' nests in the rubber trees. Sometimes they were so high that not even the strongest spices could kill their taste or smell. This treat, which turned up for children's lunch every other day, was followed by a traditional nursery pudding – frogspawn, boiled baby, squashed flies or bus accident, old Cooky's repertoire. And throughout the meal you had to keep a sharp lookout, as squirrels took flying leaps at the table, helped themselves to whatever they fancied, and were off again before you could catch them. Occasionally, unexpected contributions were added to the menu, as when a fat and meaty tail, shaken off by a lizard on a rafter above, landed in Marie's curry.

As there was no electricity in the bungalow, we had no fans. At midday the heat was unbearable. To make it possible to eat at all, the punkah was in operation throughout the meal. The youngest houseboy, stationed behind a screen, pulled a rope attached to a large palm-leaf mat which hung above the table and swung back and forth, creating a welcome breeze which cooled our streaming faces.

Our parents' lunch, which they took after ours at 2 p.m., would be our left-overs. On the rare occasions (such as birthdays) when we had a meal with them, Marie would come in with a bunch of canes, which she slipped into the crooks of our arms to make sure we sat up properly during these orgies of parental indulgence. This made eating difficult, and before long the canes were removed – probably at Papa's instigation, for my mother would never have dared defy Marie so openly – so that by the time the pudding was handed round, we would be slouching comfortably in our chairs again.

At dinner, which we ate with Marie the punkah was replaced by a roaring acetylene lamp, which produced supper for the creatures in our nursery zoo. As malaria was a constant menace, and mosquitoes were out on their rounds in clouds by the evening, we wore sarongs sewn into bags to keep the scourge off our legs during dinner. Marie, climbing into her mosquito bag respectfully held open for her by the head houseboy, was a solemn sight.

At the end of the meal we would troop upstairs, keeping well away from the banisters as usual, and, bearing our burnt-offerings of fried insects, tip-toe into the sitting-room, where Mamma would be stitching away at her embroidery and Papa playing the piano, with the usual mournful look on his Gothic features. Here was another and smaller version of the dining-room lamp, against which more insects banged noisily, casting huge, sinister shadows on the wooden partitions, which were decorated with the skins of long-dead pythons, crossed Japanese swords and Malay krises.

It was a secure and cosy scene, with the black night brooding outside, punctuated by the hooting of owls, the occasional bark of a leopard or the roar of a tiger, sinister rustling sounds, and sometimes the distant trumpeting of elephants. And always in the background, the beating of the tom-toms in the Tamil villages. We had to keep still and were not allowed to talk. We could draw or look at picture-books, as long as we turned the pages quietly.

When grown-up dinner was announced, Marie collected us to get ready for bed. We washed and undressed, then sat around the nursery table. We would go on scribbling in our drawing-books, while Marie drowsily read out items from old copies of *Planter's Weekly*, *Punch* or the *Straits Times*, which occasionally featured stories and verses written by my father. We always felt very proud of these, even though we understood no word of what she read – English was still complete gibberish to us. On and on she droned, occasionally dropping off to sleep, then waking up with a snort to resume her reading with her head on one side, her good eye aimed at the page. Then one day, to our intense amazement, we were fascinated to hear her read a perfectly intelligible account of the King of England's funeral out of the *Straits Times*. This was a revelation, a breakthrough into a new dimension. I have never understood how it happened. Suddenly, and totally without warning, an unknown language had become familiar, and we were even able to speak it.

From then on our evening sessions around the nursery table were a new experience. We learnt that Chinese pirates, sailing up the river, had forced a Tamil woman to swallow a live snake, and had cut off the fingers of several others who wouldn't hand over their rings, while a planter's wife had shaken an arm off her cook, who was riddled with jungle-rot, as well as countless other improbable stories of a similar nature. In spite of this new interest, Anne, who was only 3, would suddenly fall forwards on to her scribbling-pad with a heavy thud, and would be carried off to bed. Then Marie would start to read again, nod and snore, shake herself awake, and bundle us crossly off to bed too.

It was around this time that Anne missed an agonizing death by the skin of her teeth. The rat population, which had been growing bolder for a long time, had a habit, with which nobody interfered, of scuttling nonchalantly around the bungalow, getting to the table before us at meals, escorting us to the nursery after dinner, and baring their teeth and snarling when refused entry. The final straw came when Marie found her batch of newborn Leghorn chicks nibbled away to beak and claw. She immediately ordered poison from the Kuala Lumpur stores, and distributed slices of toast spread with cyanide all over the bungalow, under beds and wardrobes, on window ledges, and wherever else she could think of. And it was one of these poisoned crusts that Anne picked up one day, and was just about to chew when Marie snatched it from her jaws and threw it out of the window. Anne's life was saved, but it was decreed that someone had to die that day. The little household monkey, who was sitting outside popping her fleas, picked it up, and was dead within the hour.

* * *

The nights were seldom undisturbed. We were quite often woken by some unexpected commotion or disaster of one kind or another. If it was not a sudden and fearful fight among the houseboys, it might be the roar of a man-eating tiger prowling round the bungalow or the Tamil villages, or the tom-toms celebrating a birth, a death or the unexpected arrival of a relative from Southern India.

From time to time, without warning, a forest fire broke out in the middle of the night. On one unforgettable occasion we were woken up by an appalling racket – the banging of tom-toms all round the bungalow, and the most terrifying yells and screams we had ever heard. Thinking all the devils of the jungle were converging on the house, we leaped out of bed in a panic.

The factory was on fire, and thousands of tons of sheet rubber were going up in flames. There had been no rain for many months, and there was no water to put out the fire. It had to burn itself out. It was an awe-inspiring sight. A huge barrage of flames rose straight into the black sky, bursting and rattling like machine-gun fire. Papa had the gong banged for silence, and he harangued the multitude from the veranda. As he spoke in Tamil, we didn't understand much of what he said, but the main message was to chop down all the trees within reach of the blaze. And off they all went at a gallop.

The chopping and burning went on all night. Nobody thought of sending us to bed. We watched until sunrise, when the flames finally changed to black, reeking fumes, rolling slowly in the still dawn. The awful smell of burnt rubber hung about for days, making us all feel queasy and quite incapable of swallowing our curries and boiled babies.

Another fearful night, the devil whom I had tempted came out of the jungle and sat on my chest as I lay on my bed in the dark. I could blame no one but myself. Marie had warned us many times that if we ever looked into a mirror, we would see the devil sitting on our shoulder.

On one of my prowls around the bungalow, I had come across a hand mirror on my mother's dressing-table. Picking it up without much thought, I was surprised to see my face in it. Realizing what I had done, I put it down with a shudder and ran out of the room. Next day I found myself creeping back, inch by inch, to the same spot. Temptation was too strong, and I had another quick look. Not the slightest glimmer or suspicion of the devil. And I regret to say that day after day I went back to that confounded looking-glass.

The devil never appeared on my shoulder, but the night of his visit was the most terrifying experience of my life. Poor Marie, who thought I was having a fit, tried to calm me down as I thrashed about on my bed, screaming hysterically in a state of utter panic. The devil, sitting on my chest, was hacking away, trying to claw the soul out of my throat.

This little interlude ruled out all further experiments with mirrors for many years to come. The abominations were strictly banned from our living quarters. There were none in the nursery or (heaven forbid!) in the bathroom. When I next caught sight of my reflection, many years later, I was surprised to see that I was almost grown up.

Vanity was Marie's bugbear, and she was going to make sure of stamping it out before it had a chance to get a grip on us. People at the Selangor Club, to which we occasionally went, would sometimes, in the misguided hope of mollifying her well-known ferocity, pass remarks about our looks or our clothes or our good behaviour. This would immediately call forth her most severe and frosty expression, and with her piercing blue eye directed at me, she would answer in her coldest tones, 'They are plain, naughty and difficult. A regular handful, and nothing to be proud of.' And with that she would give me a sharp prod and shove me away, in case the speaker should be so unwise as to say anything nice about *me*. And so fanatical was she about this that we were very seldom allowed to wear the delicate muslin dresses that my mother enjoyed embroidering for us. 'Putting ideas into their heads,' she would mutter, as she stuffed them away in the nursery cupboard. As Titi had made her nest there, it was her chicks who eventually enjoyed our embroidered frocks, stamping around all over the delicate fabric and sleeping among their soft folds.

* * *

The reason the factory had caught fire and gone up in flames so quickly was the terribly dry state of the land and vegetation in our district. After months of searing heat, the soil was baked like pottery and parcelled out into sections with inch-wide cracks between them.

On the day when the monsoon was expected to break, we

stood outside on the lawn waiting for it. Our excitement grew as the black clouds rolled and merged like a gigantic cake mixture. Then, again and again, flashes of lightning ripped the horizon from end to end and the crashing of thunder grew closer, until it boomed and exploded overhead. Gravel rattled along the drive, and the loose red dust was blown in great sweeps up into the trees, which writhed and groaned and whimpered as huge branches were wrenched off and carried away by the wind. All life was dying. The animals went to ground, where they would be drowned in their holes and their earths by the thousand.

When the electric storm had thundered around the sky long enough, the clouds opened up and down came the rain. It was as if an ocean in the upper layers had suddenly lost its bottom and was dropping to the earth. Within a few minutes, floods were running through the ground floor of the bungalow, with the cane furniture floating out into the back yard.

The roaring of the sky increased to such a deafening clamour that you could hardly hear the claps of thunder above the general tumult. During a particularly frightening storm one year, when we were huddled at the top of the staircase watching the tables and chairs bobbing about on the swirling waters, we were called to the drawing-room and ordered to get down on our knees and pray for the house to be spared. The great mango-tree on the lawn had just received a direct hit, split down the middle by a thunderbolt. Half of it leaned over and was soon wrenched away by the wind. Marie, who had seen, in our grandparents' house in Sydney, a thunderbolt sail in through the window and scorch its way down the centre of a dinner-party table, knew all about storms and their ways. So down on our knees we went, praying for all we were worth.

Bungalows sometimes had their roofs blown off during the monsoon, but on this occasion either the terrified urgency of our prayers swayed the elements or the storm had spent its fury, for soon afterwards it settled down to steady, driving sheets of rain which went on for several days and nights, during which we seldom got much sleep. Every time we managed to doze off a new hole would appear in the nursery roof and we had to hop out and trundle our beds to a drier spot.

In the morning the ground floor was covered with stinking ooze, and heaving with worms and leeches. Small corpses were scattered everywhere. The houseboys spent most of the day scraping, brushing and swilling away the mud. When it was cleaned up, and order more or less restored, the houseboys placed saucers of milk on the floor, in strategic places, for the snakes who might pay us a visit. Mamma tried to discourage this, but Marie assured her that the snakes were not attracted by the milk, but by Papa's nightly performances of Bach, Beethoven and Wagner. As I have always heard that snakes are deaf, I don't see how Marie could have been right on this occasion.

* * *

Malaria at the end of the monsoon was responsible eventually for my learning to read, around the age of 7. From time to time, after the morning walk, Mamma would call us in for lessons. The sound of her voice was usually the signal for us to race across the garden and hide among the coffee trees until all danger was past. Fortunately for our education, after a sufficient number of bites from the female *Anopheles*, which swarmed in great clouds at this season, we succumbed to an attack of malaria. After the first few days of acute and shivering misery the quinine began to take effect, and we settled down to a period of 'low fever', singing ears and general debilitation. It was at this point that my mother saw her chance.

Helpless and shaky, we were herded into the large mosquito cage covered with netting that stood on the veranda – Mamma's version of bolting the stable door. We had no strength to resist and education caught up with us at last. We learned how to count and add up with matchsticks, and how to measure surfaces. We drew pictures of the Red Sea opening up to let Moses and his people through. And in the end, we even learned to read – in French.

After this all books were grist to my mill. I worked my way through *Les Fables de la Fontaine* and *Le Petit Larousse Illustré*, from which I picked up all sorts of fascinating information. Although I could now speak and understand English without trouble, I was surprised how difficult it was to read. In the end I taught myself with the help of *Mother Goose's Nursery Rhymes* and *Pip, Squeak and Wilfred's Annual*, pronouncing the written words aloud in various ways until I recognized them and they made sense. From then on I was launched. I had broken through to another dimension, and there seemed no end to the possibilities of happiness it would bring.

9

Ti Vali was the Tamils' annual religious festival. Around mid-day the entire workforce would gather on the lawn in front of the bungalow. We sat on garden chairs opposite the assembled company, and the headman hung garlands of hibiscus flowers around our necks. There were speeches in Tamil, followed by magic turns, and all kinds of stunts were laid on for our benefit throughout the afternoon.

I am not sure if the rope trick was ever performed at one of these shows, or if I saw it elsewhere. But one extraordinary performance was staged by a hypnotized man, who lay flat on the point of a sword which was stuck in the ground and stood straight up in the air. Stiff as a board and hardly breathing, he lay there fast asleep for the rest of the afternoon. The show went on around him, with men swallowing fire and others pushing daggers down their throats, with never a drop of blood to be seen.

I don't think fire-walking ever took place in our garden, but I remember watching it at the Selangor Club. A trench about fifteen feet long and six feet wide was dug out of the ground and filled with burning charcoal. And over this, barefoot, strolled a young man in a white sarong. He showed us his feet at the end of the stretch, and they were not even scorched.

Since then I have heard that this trick can be mastered by anyone who really wants to learn it.

Christmas was also a great time for celebrations. Although it never felt quite right in a tropical climate, we did our best to make it as convincing as possible. On Christmas Eve we would set off to the edge of the jungle in the old Fiat, armed with saws and choppers, and plunge into the undergrowth to select our tree. As there are no pines in the tropics, and most jungle trees consist of a smooth thin stem several hundred feet high, crowned with a small tuft at the top, we had to compromise and make do with the nearest thing we could find. Eventually we settled for the most likely bush, usually covered with thorns, spikes, hooks and claws, all quite useful for hanging decorations. When it was set up on the veranda under the stars, sprinkled with puffs of cotton wool, and dozens of candles flickering against the pitch-black background of the rubber trees, you could practically imagine yourself in front of the real thing.

We would all gather round as Mamma sat down at the piano and played 'O Tannenbaum', which she sang in French, while Marie piped away in German. The effect was perhaps a little unusual, but we thought it perfectly lovely, and it was moreover a tremendous relief to feel the habitual tension between the two of them easing for a few minutes.

Next morning the tree looked as if it had been hit by a hurricane. Rats, busy scrambling all over it throughout the night, had nibbled away the decorations, the nuts and the sweets, and every single candle, down to the last scrap of wax they could find. After the presents were handed out we all trooped down to the dining-room to have lunch together, as one of the special treats of the year.

In the afternoon there was a children's party at the Selangor Club where the tree, probably a fake pine brought over from Europe for the purpose, was surrounded by mountains of presents for us all. I remember Father Christmas arriving in an open car stuffed with parcels, honking his way through the surrounding jungle. Tea, a magnificent spread of Christmas cake, jam tarts, chocolates and all kinds of sweets and other delights, was much looked forward to, as these commodities were all severely rationed at home. There the only sweets we ever got were sticks of barley sugar which came out of square jars, handy for pickling centipedes and scorpions for Marie's collection. And I suspect barley sugar was only allowed because of the convenient size and shape of the jars.

Whether it was Christmas, a birthday party or any other afternoon treat, Marie dreaded our visits to the Selangor Club as much as we looked forward to them. Once there, it was impossible for her to keep us away from other children. So on the rare occasions when our parents invited us to join them, we were overjoyed. And after they and the other Club members had gone off to play golf or tennis, their little angels looked around for trouble, and drew together to commit their abominations. One of our young friends, Judy Harding, was afraid of nobody, and nothing made her squeamish. She set up blissful paddling parties in the fish-pond. And she would chop up earthworms and swallow the pieces. We followed her everywhere, regardless of the consequences. She organized visits to the kitchen, where the houseboys fed us on forbidden grown-up delicacies. And pulling down her knickers, little Judy Harding would show us her bottom for a cent a peep.

Her pluck when in pain was awe-inspiring. When she had played with a mad dog and had to have the anti-rabies injections in her stomach which we all dreaded, she could only hobble around, doubled-up in agony, but she dismissed the whole thing as if it was nothing at all. She was a great girl. Marie, however, was not impressed.

From time to time an invitation arrived for a fancy-dress party, a social occasion we dreaded beyond all others, as we hated dressing up. But my mother, who was very clever with her needle, enjoyed creating our costumes. Once, much against my will, I was dressed up as a powder-box, and Anne was the powder-puff, with bits of swan's-down stitched all over her skirt.

However embarrassed and absurd we felt in our get-up, there was no way out. As for my mother, totally unconscious of our misery, she was delighted when our costumes were a success. There were a great many pirates and fairies, but no other powder-box or powder-puff. To Marie, of course, this was nothing more than our usual showing-off and craving for attention, though in this case, attention was the last thing we wanted.

At other times, quite as unwelcome, we were dressed up in some of Mamma's daintiest creations and driven over to dancing classes in Selangor. I remember thumping my way through a loathsome number called 'Baskets of Flowers' to the tune of 'Tea for Two', ground out on an old gramophone. Feeling like an elephant with sore feet myself, I noticed Anne suddenly getting carried away, hopping up and down in her pink georgette, looking as dainty as a hibiscus flower.

Mamma made most of our everyday dresses as well, or rather she cut them out and handed them over to the Chinese tailor who came once a month to finish them off. But apart from this, and her embroidery, she had very little to do, and time must have dragged for her. The rich life of the garden and the jungle, which sustained us entirely, meant very little to her. All her interests lay in people and human contact. Given the chance, she could have talked forever. Papa's un-relenting silences must have been very frustrating. In the evenings, when they lay on their *chaises longues* before dinner with their whiskies, and my father was buried in a book, she would hazard a few remarks, which were invariably answered in the same way: 'Mmm?' And she had to be content with this, as nothing else ever came. During the day she played the piano a great deal. Chopin was her favourite; and we were turned inside out when she played and sang Gounod's 'Ave Maria'. To this day it sends shivers down my spine just to remember it. She also knew all the French popular *chansons*, music and words, by heart, and these she sang when, forget-ting she was British, nostalgia for her country overwhelmed her.

These songs were mostly stirring and patriotic and had a good deal to do with devotion to duty and heroic death. Some of them reduced us to tears. There was one in which a poor carrier-pigeon, flying over German-occupied Alsace, was shot in the breast by a fiendish soldier but flew on, bleeding slowly to death, until he reached his post and delivered his message, dying in the hands of the officer who received him. Another described the harrowing end of a young girl dying of consumption, while her small brother, believing that she would die when the last autumn leaf touched the ground, spent his time trying to catch them as they fell.

Clustered on pouffes around Mamma at the piano, we were stirred to the ends of our toes by her clear high voice and the sadness of the songs, and great tears rolled down our cheeks. Then, feeling thoroughly set up by this orgy of sentimentality, and with the unconscious but implacable cruelty of children, we left her to her own tears and clattered down the stairs to race round the garden with the low-flying swallows or bats.

* * *

Sometimes, when the worst heat of the day was over, we all climbed into the old Fiat and set off for Jeram, our favourite beach on the west coast. This fishing village, a few huts on stilts at the mouth of a river, numbered a dozen or so Malay families whose entire livelihood came from the sea. Everywhere rotting fish bones lay in piles, over which flies buzzed in dense masses.

We drove past the huts towards the long white beach lined with mangroves and coconut trees, some of which grew right down to the edge of the water. The warm sea in which we wallowed was full of life of every kind. It swarmed with crabs and small, extraordinary fish that crawled out of the water and hopped about all over the beach, puffing themselves up to the size of a golf-ball. These were so numerous and generally popular that they were made into toys and sold in all the bazaars of the area. There was also a kind of prehistoric-looking shellfish with a long razor-sharp tail. The fishermen said there was a poison in the end of the tail which either killed you outright or gave you four days of high fever. The Malays cooked these 'handbag crabs', as we called them, on the beach for their supper, placing them upside-down on the flames like frying pans. Their eggs, bright-red and the size of peas, were picked out and eaten one by one.

But most curious of all was a species of silver-coloured fish that wobbled out of the water on their fins. Hopping across the sand, they shinned up the first coconut tree they came across. I have never discovered what they did when they got to the top. Perhaps, like salmon, they returned to their birthplace to spawn, and the trees were crowned with their nests.

The shallows in which we splashed and paddled were heaving with sea-snakes wriggling around in the foam. No one ever went into the water without a couple of stones to hurl in self-defence. I made a direct hit once, catching a couple which were gracefully weaving around each other by my knees. The waves suddenly ran red with blood. This put me off bathing for quite a long time. Although these snakes were supposed to be as deadly as cobras, we never had any serum with us – there was probably no such thing at the time. And anyway, the stones we carried seemed magically to protect us, as none of us was ever bitten.

There were snakes in the sand as well, so that the delightful pastime of digging and castle-building lost some of its appeal. At dusk we sat on logs of driftwood and watched the swarms of hermit crabs popping out of the sand and dragging their shells down to the sea. After paddling about in the Indian Ocean for a while, they scrambled out again and fussily dug themselves back into their holes.

When the sky began to turn crimson, as the sun dipped into the sea on the horizon, we all climbed back into the car for the long drive home to Assam Java through the gloom of the darkening jungle. And we were limp and drugged with sleep when we finally arrived back at the bungalow.

* * *

Although we loved our garden and the daily walks through the estate, the monthly visits to Kuala Lumpur were a great treat, in spite of the agonies of car-sickness. And because our parents would never allow the car to stop in the jungle, the dogs and I, crammed into the front seat, spent most of the journey hanging over the side being sick into the wind.

On one of these trips we suddenly saw a large cobra snaking its way out of the ditch towards the road. The snake and Sandenam, the chauffeur, caught sight of each other at the same time, and both instantly put on a terrific turn of speed. They met head-on in the middle of the road, with the front wheels cutting the snake into three pieces. There was a thump and a hideous crunching sound as the tail came whipping up the side of the car. Sandeman whooped with glee, and I was sick once more at the sight and sound of it all.

But as soon as I staggered on to firm ground again I recovered very quickly. We got out at the Majestic Hotel and swept up the front steps, feeling very grand. They were so different from our own shaky, worm-eaten staircase at home, festooned with centipedes and spiders, and for ever threatening to collapse under our feet.

A houseboy, gleaming and crackling with starch, led us to a large bedroom with a private bath and its very own veranda. After soaking in pure, clear water (no stinking rubber slime here) we changed into fresh clothes and were marched down the corridor to the barber's shop. By then feeling quite well again, I was looking forward to the pleasures of the day.

The hair-cutting session was a boring but necessary evil, though the feel of the clippers on the back of the neck, which sent shivers down the spine, was quite a pleasant sensation. When this was over we set out into the glaring heat, which slapped you in the face like a hot pancake. We climbed into a rickshaw for our usual drive around the town and the ritual visit to Whiteway Laidlaw's stores to restock on our crayons and painting materials, while Marie bought yards of elastic for our silk bloomers, cotton for the sewing-machine, and fresh supplies of a special ointment called Zambuk, which cured all ills. Stowing these treasures away in the rickshaw, we told our runner to take us to the river, our favourite spot in town. There we spent the rest of the morning watching the coming and going of the water traffic, the loading and unloading of sampans, rolling up of fishing-nets and sorting out of catches, and men and beasts at their ablutions. It was comforting to see our rickshaw man sitting at peace under a tree, getting his wind back, enjoying the rest and knowing he was getting paid for it. It was common knowledge that he and his colleagues had all had their spleens taken out, so they could run for miles without getting puffed. Until one day, without warning, they would drop dead between the shafts.

Elephants shambled up to the river and stepped daintily into the murky shallows, where they let themselves down carefully on their knees like arthritic charwomen, then rolled over on one side to wallow in the warm mud. Their little boy keepers, only about 5 years old, climbed on to their bulging flanks and set to work with scrubbing-brushes. Meanwhile the great beasts obligingly squirted jets of water to rinse away the loosened dirt, enjoying the scratch and tickle and the attention.

We would rejoin our parents at the Majestic for two o'clock lunch. Marie attended these meals without her hat, which made her feel terribly underdressed. To make up for it, she wore a wide silver-studded black velvet ribbon around her neck. Her blue-and-white check uniform was so stiffly starched that it stood out around her like a parachute. On these occasions, for some obscure reason, she felt it was 'her place' to speak only German, and pretend to understand no other language.

On one of these Kuala Lumpur expeditions I was taken straight to the hospital instead of the hotel. As nothing had been said, I was terrified when a nurse took me by the hand and dragged me away from Marie. Whimpering and trembling, I was led to a wide veranda overlooking a paved garden, with a pond full of long-tailed Japanese goldfish and a small fountain dribbling over them. Banana trees trailed their leaves over the edge, giant orchids smouldered on their stalks, creepers hung like green hair from the palm trees, and the hibiscus bushes throbbed with a multitude of humming birds. Here I was dumped on a bed surrounded by powerful overhead lights and instruments that looked like praying mantises aiming their alarming prongs at my face. A mask came down over my mouth, and I clawed at it in panic. They managed to fix it on at last, with three nurses holding me down, while I screamed and struggled in a state of absolute terror, until the gas mercifully did its work and I passed out. When I finally came round, one of the nurses was holding up a small object covered with blood on the end of a pair of tweezers.

'There you are,' she said, 'there's your tooth. And you never felt a thing, did you?' I stared at it in amazement. All that fuss, fear and panic for pulling out one miserable tooth! I liked to imagine afterwards that I might have behaved better if they had told me what was going to happen. But I couldn't be sure.

An undeserved reward was waiting for me on the back seat of the car – a beautiful doll, almost as large as myself, with a delicate china face, eyes that opened and closed, and legs that bent. I kept her carefully through my teens, and somehow throughout the upheavals of the war as well, hoping that one day I would have a daughter of my own, who would treasure her as much as I did. But by the time this came about, fashionable dolls were made of pink plastic, with fibreglass wigs and high pointing bosoms. Mine belonged to a different world.

* * *

On another occasion, after a period of prolonged disobedience and misbehaviour on our part, it was decided to give us a good fright. There was a boarding-school in Kuala Lumpur that Marie had told us about, which she said served as a kind of prison for unruly children. We had been threatened with this on several occasions, and now it seemed the time had come to do something about it. So on our next visit to Kuala Lumpur we were bundled into a rickshaw and off we set in fearful trepidation to visit our would-be jail.

The building itself, all red brick and corrugated tin, was forbidding enough. But the surrounding garden more than made up for it. Filled with purple hibiscus, banana trees in bloom, and palms smothered in flowering orchids, it was a living paradise. Brightly coloured birds and enormous butterflies flapped around in great numbers. And on the lawn was a group of Chinese and Eurasian children playing a lively game of blind man's buff.

Apart from the head nun who came out to greet us, we saw no other European. She was completely charming, and moved with great dignity and purpose, like a well-trimmed ship. She showed us round the school, and we followed her through the classrooms, the dormitories, the dining-room and kitchen. From time to time we asked, 'And where is the prison?' or 'When can we see your jail?' At which Marie growled, 'Be quiet and behave yourselves.'

At the end of our visit, the nun led us to a large cupboard and handed out a brand-new toy to each of us. I forget what John and Anne got, but I was given a mechanical monkey pulling a barrow-load of mangosteens. Feeling puzzled and thoroughly confused, we thanked her politely, and Marie conducted us back to our rickshaw in silence. There was no more talk of boarding-school after that. Back we went to Assam Java, to our wicked ways and blissful existence.

10

Two or three times a year, when we felt even more crushed by the heat than usual, the family would retreat to 'the Hills' to cool off. We would drive to Bukit Fraser, a holiday station up in the mountains where Europeans from all over the peninsula retreated whenever they could spare the time. For us this meant two or three glorious weeks, a change of routine and, most appealing of all, the chance of meeting 'other children'. We were always dispatched in advance with the luggage, after which Sandenam would return to collect our parents two or three days later.

We would set off at dawn, before the heat of the day settled on the plain. The old Fiat was loaded to the roof with trunks, cases and picnic hampers packed with cold jungle fowl, hard-boiled duck eggs, baskets of fruit and flasks of lukewarm lime-juice. Much of our menagerie was on board as well. This included the dogs, a mongoose or two (in case of cobras), the little monkey and Titi the hen. Various invalids were strapped in their splints, the tortoises scrabbled in their cardboard box, and there were the inevitable jars of tarantulas and scorpions, as the servants couldn't be trusted to look after them at home. The dogs and I always sat in the front, as we were invariably sick as soon as we began to lurch round the hairpin bends.

The journey took all day. Somewhere halfway up the mountain, and strictly against the rules, Marie gave orders to stop for lunch. A suitable spot was found by the roadside, rugs were spread out and the hampers unpacked. Native fashion, we used banana leaves as plates. On one occasion, turning my head I looked straight into the sulky face of a full-grown orang-utan. A little nervously, we threw him some bananas. He picked them up and shambled away.

We would arrive after dark and unload by torchlight. The nights were much cooler than on the plain, and it was delicious luxury to snuggle into pullovers and woolly scarves. Our happiness would have overflowed if it had suddenly started to snow.

On one of these visits our cousins, who were so wild they had to have a man to look after them instead of the usual *amah*, were staying at the guesthouse when we arrived. We all behaved so badly that Marie immediately rented a small house on the edge of the jungle and transferred us to it with all our kit, the dogs, the bottled spiders and the rest of the menagerie. But it turned out to be a case of out of the frying-pan, as a panther prowled around the house every night in search of an open window. We had no idea how long the shutters would survive when charged by a two-hundredweight battering-ram of hungry panther. The houseboys assured us that big cats didn't much like child meat, although they would make do with it if nothing else was available. In this case it was probably the dogs they were after.

The best time of day at Bukit Fraser was the early morning,

when huge warm clouds of steam rolled out of the jungle, and the air was so sodden with mist you could almost scoop up the moisture in your hands. The pugmarks of bears that had padded around the house during the night proved how close they had come. When after a short early morning trek we came back for breakfast, which we took with the adults, we were greeted by the most delicious smells in the world – smoked haddock, fried bacon or kippers. Here at Bukit Fraser we had a real English cooked breakfast for the first time in our lives. Even the coarse and lumpy porridge was welcome and satisfying.

After breakfast came the jungle walks, infinitely more eventful than our tame mornings around Assam Java. On one occasion we walked down the mountain in search of a giant death's-head moth which lived in the darkest part of the forest. For several hours we struggled through the most impenetrable vegetation we had ever seen. Giant monkey cups, enormous tree-ferns wrapped in creepers and climbing orchids struggled for space with huge scaly palms entangled in lianas like fishing-nets. By then we were covered with leeches clamped on to our bare arms and legs, while their hind-quarters, filled with blood, waved up and down behind them like tassels. And there they had to stay until we got back. For if you tear a leech off your skin you go on bleeding: only they can seal off the wound with their spit, to keep the remaining blood supply intact for future needs.

Suddenly Marie realized we had lost our way. The opening we had made through the jungle had closed behind us. We were about to turn back on what we hoped were our tracks when the sound of browsing elephants could suddenly be heard among the trees. Frozen with fear, we stopped dead and stared at Marie. The sounds of tearing and wrenching, munching, rumbling and belching were approaching. I wondered why Marie didn't make us run for it. So far the herd was unaware of our presence, and I thought we could have got away, as the elephants were moving very slowly. But she probably assumed they would hear us crashing through the undergrowth and that this would enrage them. She knew the sudden anger of disturbed elephants and their terrifying reaction to unexpected intrusion, particularly if they have young with them, when they trample and tear apart everything in their path.

We stood there dead still, hardly daring to breathe, for an extremely long time. At last, gradually and very slowly, the sounds began to recede. The elephants had turned aside, and were moving in another direction. We kept quite still until they were out of hearing.

Miraculously, the stress seemed to restore Marie's sense of direction, and we found our way home in silence, without seeing our death's-head, but with a multitude of unwanted leeches instead. It took us a long time to ease them off with salt, as we couldn't bring ourselves to sizzle them up with cigarette-ends, which would have been much quicker. That day we fell on our lunch with more than our usual voracity. There is nothing like a good strong Madras curry for setting you up after a fright.

On our next expedition into the thickest part of the jungle, Marie was taking no more chances, and she hired a guide for the day. This time we were after human quarry. She wanted to see the Sakais, the last of the aboriginal tribes who have been living in the jungles of the Malayan peninsula since prehistoric times and haven't changed since then.

These naked, diminutive people, sometimes described as 'forest dwarves', have survived all the efforts of successive invaders to eliminate them. The Sakais now live in small nomadic groups, spread out all over the jungle, isolated from one another and from the rest of humanity. They have found this the most successful way of life for continued survival. Living entirely on the resources of their surroundings, they hunt and ward off enemies with blow-pipes and poisoned arrows, which they have been using since earliest times. The darts are dipped in the sap of the upas-tree, the lethal qualities of which last for a couple of months. As the Sakais know how to remain invisible, and their arrows are shot through a hollow tube in complete silence, it is impossible to find them unless they decide to show themselves. According to legend, they have learnt how to vanish on the spot, a trick they picked up in order to escape from the Hantu Hutan, the evil spirits of the jungle.

There are innumerable theories on the origins and present way of life of the Sakais. So Marie decided to find out what she could for herself, and off we set in the wake of our guide for the day. Following in his footsteps, we scrambled through a barrage of leaves and creepers so dense that a fly would have had trouble finding a way through. But our man hacked to right and left with his machete, and we wriggled on.

We came across several sites where fires had been hastily stamped out, but although we searched the clearings and scrutinized the trees, we saw nothing more than the odd python, a couple of sloths hanging upside down fast asleep with their claws wrapped around a branch, and a few bats snoozing the day away. There was not a glimmer of a Sakai. The guide told us that they were definitely around. As they obviously had no wish to materialize, however, we never caught a glimpse of them. And to this day we still don't know what a Sakai looks like. It was a great disappointment.

For some mysterious reason, it was always in the hills that the miseries of jungle rot came to a festering head. The trouble, which started with the slightest scratch or cut, was held in abeyance on the plain with regular applications of Zambuk, our magic cure-all ointment. But as soon as we arrived at Bukit Fraser, its power dwindled and the rot spread with alarming speed.

The daily visits to the local chemist for dressings were torture, and would have been quite unbearable but for one bright spot. On the counter, among the cough mixtures, the purges and the aphrodisiacs (snakes' guts from Assam Java?), sat an enormous horny, mottled toad as large as a pumpkin, preserved in a jar of meths. This ineffably beautiful and desirable creature kept our spirits up throughout the ordeal of the dressings. Marie eyed it as enviously as we did. And on the last day of our visit to the hills, she came out of the shop bearing the jar with the toad inside it. I have no idea how she managed to persuade the Chinese chemist to part with his treasure. But it came back to Assam Java with us and took the place of honour on the nursery shelves. Zambuk's power was restored, and our horrible jungle rot, of which I still have the scars on my elbows and ankles, simmered down to manageable levels again.

* * *

Back at Assam Java, life seemed rather tame and flat after our exciting jaunts around Bukit Fraser. Our first outing after our return would usually be a visit to church. And this was no great treat.

The service was held in a wooden hut with a tin roof, on to which rubber seeds raining out of the trees above bounced and rattled like grapeshot. We sat on rickety benches in two rows near the altar, while the congregation, which the priest had managed to capture that morning, crouched on the earthen floor, chewing betel nut and spewing thin red jets of spit several feet in front of them. But kindly and considerate as they were, these people aimed at the spaces between the heads, and nobody was ever hit.

The air was hot and steamy, and infinitely smelly. There was no music, no hymns, just the monotonous chanting of the priest, and the nasal responses of the congregation. It was a relief to get outside and find that small booths and shop-windows strapped to bicycle handlebars had arrived just in time to catch us at the end of the service. As this was our only chance in the week to spend our pocket-money, we made a bee-line for them. There were tiny celluloid models of tigers, elephants and the small puffer fish that hopped about on the beaches all round the coast. And various carved and hand-painted miniature objects – Japanese dolls in kimonos and complicated hair-dos, Chinese sunshades made of oiled paper, bamboo flutes, silk parachutes strapped to toy monkeys, and a multitude of glass bangles of every possible colour. You could get the latter for a cent a dozen. John frequently bought great numbers of them. One day Mamma asked him who they were for.

'They are for my daughters,' he said briefly.

'Oh, you are going to have daughters?'

'Yes,' he replied, 'I am going to have four.' And he did, in due course, have the four very charming daughters for whom he had been collecting bangles since the age of 5.

II

One fine day, without any explanation or warning, Marie announced: 'We are going back to Vence, and I want you to sort out your toys.'

Coming out of the blue as it did, it was quite a shock. When we recovered, we realized that what she was really saying was, 'You will have to give most of your treasures away.' Then she added, 'You can just keep a few of your favourite things. I want you to put them on your beds straight after breakfast, as they will have to be packed by the end of the day.'

We collected as many of our dearest belongings as would fit on our beds, knowing quite well that only a few would be picked out for packing, and all the rest given away to the estate children. But as the thought of going back to Mas Mistral filled us with excitement, parting with most of our possessions seemed small hardship. The only disappointment about returning to Europe was that our father was staying behind. Once more we would be parted from him for months, perhaps even years.

The sad day came only too soon. Apart from a few innocuous storms the voyage back was uneventful, and we never got the shipwreck we were all secretly hoping for.

Soon after our arrival at Mas Mistral, Mamma disappeared

one day without saying goodbye. As there was nothing unusual in this, we took it in our stride. What did surprise us was the arrival of an unexpected guest, who had apparently come to look after us during Mamma's absence. As Marie had always done this job, we were much relieved that she was apparently staying on. We had no real objection to Mrs G's arrival, especially as she came equipped with a small daughter of our own age, and a delightful chow who joined in all our games. But Marie's nose was severely put out of joint.

John, who had recently seen a blind man being led by a guide dog in Nice, decided to train the poor chow for the job, in case one of us should suddenly need it. Day after day, we would come across them padding round the garden, Fang with his black tongue hanging out of his mouth in utter boredom, and John with his eyes tight shut, hanging on to the dog's collar. This went on until the poor creature, finally overcome by the July heat, thirst and general exhaustion, suddenly turned and nicked a small chunk out of John's left ear. Not surprisingly, there was a good deal of blood. Marie always maintained that ear lobes were little bags of reserve blood, like spare fat in a camel's hump. From that moment on, poor Fang had to be chained up, as the fear of rabies was always uppermost in people's minds. And according to Marie, this was most likely to strike during the hot summer months, when milk turned sour in the human breast and dogs went mad.

In Molly, Mrs G's daughter, we at last had a companion on the spot. John and his damaged ear were removed to another room, and Moll, as we called her, joined Anne and myself in the night nursery. It was pure joy to have a friend on tap day and night, and we chattered excitedly for hours. No punishment, however severe, could stop our endless flow.

Mrs G wandered in and out of the nursery as she pleased, which was another cause of aggravation for poor Marie, for she regarded this as her own exclusive preserve. Mrs G was a tall, desiccated woman dressed in the colonial style, in long white calico skirts and white cotton stockings, with a little tail of white chiffon hanging from the back of her hat. She was kind, serene and equable, and for the first time in our lives we received a daily ration of chocolate – minute red-wrapped slabs, enclosing a picture, which we saved up to stick into a book specially made for the purpose. When one of these books was filled up, the grocer exchanged it for a toy which we were allowed to choose from the storeroom at the back of the shop. Marie deplored this wanton spoiling and could hardly wait for Mrs G, her Molly and her chocolate rations to depart.

One very hot afternoon in early August we were ordered upstairs and kitted out in our best white clothes, then bundled into one of Papa's buses bound for Nice. And there we were taken to a nursing home, where we were amazed to find Mamma lying in bed with a cradle beside her, containing, we were told, our new baby sister.

When they finally came home, Christine was installed in Marie's bedroom, which became the new night nursery. Her baby days were spent in the wobbly old pram under the cherry tree on the terrace. But in spite of constant and devoted attention, our new sister did a terrible lot of screaming, especially at night. The noise was so loud and overpowering that, as her lungs grew in strength, it drowned out the sound of Marie's snores, to which I had become so accustomed that they no longer woke me up.

This went on night after night, and eventually I crept down the corridor in the dark to see what I could do about it. I felt sure that Christine must be desperately unhappy. I rocked her, shook her and tried whistling to her, all without success. Until eventually I hit on a magic formula, which worked from then on without fail. Leaning over her cot, I blew on her face, which surprised her into instant silence – until I ran out of breath, when she set up her howling again. So night after night, for what seemed like months, I managed to keep her quiet. Although by the time I staggered back to bed I felt dazed, and my head was spinning and aching, I thought it was well worth the effort to stop that appalling noise. From then on I applied the method whenever and wherever necessary, and the family regarded my influence over Christine with some awe. But I carefully concealed my tactics, as instinct warned me they might not meet with complete approval.

When this new pride and joy was old enough to stand and waddle around, Marie dug out of the Australian trunks in the attic the delicate, exquisitely tucked and embroidered Edwardian dresses trimmed with lace that my Aunt Mimi had worn half a century earlier under the skies of the Southern Cross. And we became accustomed to the sight of Christine's short, square, sturdy figure stumping around under the mimosa trees, dressed in flounces of white lace flowing down to the ground and flapping around her fat ankles. I came across her once, decked out in all this finery, in a bed of Madonna lilies, standing on tiptoe, holding my paint-box in one hand and splashing with red paint the white waxy trumpets of the lilies, which she could only just reach. The poor things, she explained, had been left out by the Almighty when he dealt out their colours to the flowers of the garden. She was a pious child, and her mind turned naturally to divine intercourse whenever the need arose. Once, when the three of us were due for a routine visit to the dentist in Nice, my mother found her on her knees in Marie's bedroom, praying fervently for Anne to be struck down by some sudden and fearful illness, so that she would have to stay behind and keep her company.

Christine, who knew her own mind from the start, was firm in everything she said or did, and the only human being in my experience who could stand up to Marie and get away with it. She simply said No, she would *not* eat her porridge or her spinach, and if the plate wasn't whisked away at once, she rapped the table with her spoon, and Marie came to heel at once. It was incredible. If we had tried these tactics ourselves, a sharp smack would have been the answer.

'La *vieille et la jeune*', Marie would say, as they pottered about hand in hand all day long, picking raspberries for the table, checking the linen cupboards, feeding the hens and an ever-increasing army of cats which came from far afield, word having got round since our return from Malaya that there was open house at Mas Mistral again. And from time to time, at dead of night, there was a fearful commotion in the hen-house and you could hear them, Christine with a pop-gun and Marie with her air-rifle, taking pot-shots at the poachers who were raiding the *basse-cour*. These were literally shots in the dark, and I am sure that nothing was ever hit, but it served the purpose of frightening away the thieves.

We could not help feeling a little left out, as the two of them, entirely absorbed in each other, paid scant attention to anyone else. But we felt no resentment, as our devotion to Christine was absolute. Strict and bossy though she was, she looked to us like an angel, and we wove daisy-chains to decorate her blonde curls. Queening it regally in her high-chair, she accepted this admiration with calm graciousness as her due, and sat patiently while Marie twisted her hair stiffly around a candle to make the curls last longer. These long sausage curls were always known as *anglaises*.

By the time she was 3, this mane of blonde curls was the cause of one of the great uproars with which life was punctuated from time to time. On a sweltering hot July day, when not a breath of air stirred the leaves of the trees, and the grasses steamed and fermented, while the birds hopped around panting with their beaks wide open, Mamma slyly abducted Christine and carried her off to the barber in the village, where she was shorn like a French poodle, with a tuft left on top and a couple of hideous flaps at the sides, but the back shaved like a peasant boy's head. Her chubby face, no longer angel-like, looked like a swollen poppy-bud perched on the thin stalk of her neck.

'She will feel much cooler now,' said Mamma uncertainly, as she pushed the little monstrosity towards us. We were struck dumb with horror at the enormity of the sacrilege, and saw that Marie was going to 'have an attack'. But to our relief, she went to have it in her room. Her one eye shrunk to a pinhead of fury, she scooped Christine up and turned on her heel, and we saw nothing more of either of them for the next two days. After that, Christine's hair was allowed to grow again, and nobody interfered with it any more. Mamma had shot her bolt, and her fit of courage had spent itself.

Having done her job producing Christine, poor Mamma was once more casting around for something to do, and she remembered our education. With a huge Montessori book on her lap, she gathered us at her feet on the nursery floor and handed out great piles of wooden blocks to us, without suggestions or instructions of any kind. And there we sat, perplexed, wondering what we were meant to do with them. In the end, the answer didn't seem to lie in playing with bricks, and Montessori was discarded. It was then that our first governess appeared.

Grimly pious Mademoiselle C was a typical example of what my father called a 'church rat'. She made the Almighty seem like some awful kind of headmaster hanging about in the sky, waiting to catch you out and pounce with fearful retribution. A thin gaunt figure, always dressed in black bombazine, she was the ex-headmistress of a girls' school. Her fierce grey hair, which fitted her head like a stocking, was done up at the back into a mean, aggressive little bun which made you sigh just to look at it. Every few seconds her nose twitched like a rabbit's, drawing up one side of her lip and exposing the gleam of a menacing eye-tooth. A stiff black moustache bristled on her upper lip like a third eyebrow. And most off-putting of all, she had a whistling nostril which emitted a thin sound, like a faint hiss of steam, whenever she inhaled under stress. As soon as the nostril began to hiss, we knew there was about to be an explosion.

Mlle C's only redeeming feature was an ancient cat, which followed her like a dog. He had a mania for wine-bottle corks, and always had one clamped between his dribbling jaws. He sat in the middle of the table while we had our lessons, chewing his cork, and although he looked a bit like Giles's Granny, we found him a great comfort during our daily ordeal.

Unlike Marie, who was probably just as strict, Mlle C was totally unlovable. Our religious education was not her responsibility, but she took it over on arrival, so that we were completely under her thumb on every front. Our cosy Sunday sessions in the side-chapel, with Papa rustling *The Times* and John and I smuggling in the odd conker when in season, were done away with. There was no more going to church with our parents and Rubio and Marie. Bit by bit we lost our *joie de vivre*, and Marie nearly had a nervous breakdown. Mamma locked herself up in the summer study and we hardly ever saw her.

Our day started at 7 a.m., when Marie woke us up and we washed and dressed at top speed. Fifteen minutes later Mlle C stalked in for prayers. After that we trooped downstairs for bread and cocoa. The bread was stale, as Mlle C maintained that fresh bread was indigestible and lay heavy on the stomach, interfering with concentration and keenness. As it was, we were so poorly endowed with these qualities anyway that we could not afford to lose the minutest available scrap. By eight o'clock we were sitting down to work.

Mlle C covered the table with sheets of newspaper to protect it; they puckered and creased under our books. Then she uncorked a bottle of purple ink and handed each of us a pen with a thin scratchy nib, the needle-sharp, pointed ends of which crossed over with a vicious twist as soon as they touched the paper, flicking sprays of purple ink all round. If this happened too often we got a sharp rap on the knuckles with a black ruler. My copy-books were punctured with small holes and sprinkled with ink spots on every page. Most mornings ended in tears. At five minutes to twelve, Pauvre Claire crept in to lay the table, and Marie whisked us away for a quick wash and brush-up. Although she was as grim and rough as could be, we knew quite well that her bad temper had nothing to do with us.

Lunch was eaten in silence, except for the odd sniffle from whoever was still struggling with the last tears of the morning. As children were meant to be seen but not heard, Mlle C had to eat in silence too. That at least was a mercy. There was usually one of us who was made to go without pudding as a punishment, which we minded much less than being kept in during break. As we got only half an hour in the garden after lunch, our school-day seemed very long. Mamma once had the temerity to complain that I had not been out of the house for a week. She was asked not to interfere, and reminded that children have to grow pale over their books if education is to be taken seriously. Which we did, in quite a short time.

John had withdrawn into complete silence, and Anne's huge oyster-coloured eyes were usually swimming with tears. I became more neurotic as the weeks went by, caught sight of ghosts and devils on the stairs as we went to bed, and sneezed non-stop through a spring which seemed to have no end. This rule of terror lasted one whole terrible year. The day of reckoning came one fine June morning when my mother burst into the dining-room without even knocking, while we were sweating over a dictation. 'Come on, children,' she cried, 'the cherries are ripe and must be picked at once or the birds will eat them all.'

There was a terrible silence, while we stared at her as if she had gone out of her mind.

Mlle C's nostril whistled like a steam engine and then she exploded: 'I must ask you, Madame, not to disturb my pupils.'

'They must come at once,' babbled Mamma. 'Those cherries must be picked right away or we will lose the best ones.'

There was a clash of voices raised in anger, and we fled into the garden.

Gino and Marius had placed ladders against the cherry trees, and we lost no time scrambling up. We could reach the topmost branches, and we were expert pickers. The birds came fluttering angrily down, aiming at our eyes. But we held our own and ignored their bullying. John ate almost as many cherries as he picked, and that night he was so ill that he nearly died. His stomach swelled and his temperature rose, while his eyes, like a dying dog's, turned upwards. We were terrified. Marie lit a candle and made us kneel down beside him to pray for his recovery. By the morning he was better, and another two days saw him on his feet again. During which time a miracle had occurred. Mlle C had disappeared and we were *free*. This was the start of a new life – in fact we had a great many exciting new lives, starting at frequent, if unexpected, intervals.

At about this time our English neighbours, the Hilliers, who had decided to go back to England, were looking for a home for their old spaniel. Sam, a friendly and exuberant dog, was perfectly happy with life in general, except for one thing. He loathed and despised French dogs. He savaged them whenever he got the chance. This was quite a disadvantage, and nobody else was keen on giving him a home. So, what with one thing and another, Mrs Hillier was very anxious he should come to us. We begged Mamma, who was in two minds about it, to take him on. In the end she gave in, dear old Sam joined the family, and we were overjoyed at having a dog again.

That summer Mamma decided that after such a gruelling year we needed a proper holiday. Letters of enquiry went off in various directions and finally, one fine evening in early July, we set off for Nice station in a convoy of taxis. Mamma headed the column, Marie followed in the second cab with us,

Rubio captained the third, and the luggage came last. This included trunks and hampers, rugs and tents, primus stoves and tricycles, Mamma's cameras and developing kit – and most important of all, our pharmacy and medical supplies. We might have been heading for the Kalahari Desert for all we knew. In fact we were on our way to the west coast, to enjoy the iodine-laden air of the Atlantic Ocean.

At Nice station we climbed into the night train, surrounded by an army of porters, and our gear was finally loaded on board amid much shouting and excitement. Marie tied nets over our heads to keep the soot out of our hair, while simultaneously clinging on to Mamma's very obvious jewellery case. Mamma reclined on one seat, with her head wrapped up in lavender tulle, while Rubio, who had to sleep in another compartment, clasped to his bosom a heavy wooden chest filled with table silver and labelled in black letters: '*Argenterie. Service de table*'.

The picnic we had that night was heaven – the hampers were stuffed with delicacies from Madame Rose's kitchen. This was a never-to-be-forgotten treat after our long year of bread and butter and cocoa suppers. Sitting primly in our flowered pyjamas, we chewed our way through little slabs of *bifteck en croûte*, and squabs wrapped in vine leaves. There were screw-top jars of ratatouille, and scalding chicken broth drunk out of silver mugs which burnt your fingers and your lips. Plum and cherry tarts and raspberry puffs rounded things off, and then, to our surprise and delight, we were each allowed an inch of Papa's best rosé in our Vichy water. This was a rare treat, as wine, along with vinegar, was generally held to bend your bones and dissolve the teeth in your head before they even showed up.

By the time we had flicked the last crumb off our swollen bellies, it was nearing midnight. We climbed into our bunks, and Anne and I lay side by side, leaning on our elbows and watching the inky Mediterranean slipping by, edged in the west by the lime-green sky, darkening gradually to pitch-black at the top.

Swaying wildly from side to side, as French trains always did in those days, we thundered along the coast, tearing through Cagnes, Antibes, La Napoule and St Tropez, for this was the Rapide Nice-Bordeaux, not our little coastal train which stopped at every station. Fiery sparks streaked past the window, the whistle shrieked practically non-stop, telegraph wires leapt and plunged up and down, and we rolled over on our bunks and fell asleep.

Part II

THE ROAD TO BORDEAUX

1930–1940

12

The journey took all night. We arrived in Royan in good order, and the station-master, who had been alerted on the phone by the Nice *chef-de-gare*, was on the platform to meet us. Our luggage was hoisted on to a caravan of horse-drawn carriages lined up outside the station waiting for customers. We climbed into the first, a *calèche* of ancient design with tufts of horse-hair sprouting from the seats, and the tattered remains of a hood which flapped in the breeze. Rubio, still clutching the case of table-silver, climbed into the second coach with some of the luggage and immediately fell asleep.

The drive along the front of this fashionable resort was a revelation. We had never seen such enormous waves, with breakers as high as horses galloping up the beach. Dead jelly-fish as large as bicycle wheels, left stranded by the previous tide, were lifted up and floated away, to be churned and pounded by the next breaker. How could anyone bathe or even paddle in such a raging sea? 'It will be much calmer in St Georges,' said our coachman to cheer us up. 'The beach is much more sheltered there.'

We arrived at the nearby harbour village of St Georges de Didonne at the height of the shopping hour, with the market in full swing. Our convoy, shambling along the main street, caused an unexpected stir. We found this puzzling, as we looked no different from usual – if anything on the tidier side, for before leaving the train Marie had scrubbed and brushed us. It must have been Rubio who was letting us down, fast asleep in his barouche with his bristly red face squashed on to his chest, his beret over his nose, and the box of silver still firmly clasped in his arms. After him came three more coaches loaded with luggage. On top of the last one were half a dozen mouse-traps wobbling rather ominously astride our two Singer sewing-machines (in case one broke down).

Châlet Gaudin had been described by the agents as a large family residence full of old-world charm. The operative word was old. It was in fact crumbling. When our convoy stopped at the gate, we thought we had arrived at the Sleeping Beauty's castle. You could hardly see the house for the trees. They towered above the roof, vines and creepers swarmed all over the walls, and the wide front steps sweeping up to the first-floor terrace were shrouded in ferns and mosses. Great loops of cobwebs hung about like washing lines; some of the shutters were hanging from one hinge, while others were encrusted on to the walls like barnacles. The vapours of the ocean, Marie said, were the cause of it all.

Rubio, still fast asleep in the second carriage, was now prodded awake by our coachman, who poked him in the ribs with his whip. 'Come on, lazy-bones, give us a hand with the luggage,' he growled.

Unloading our bags and boxes was no joke. Apart from the trunks full of bed- and table-linen and kitchen equipment which Marie had thought it essential to bring, the load piling up in the garden included camp-beds, a field medical chest, a large box full of photographic developing material, and trunks stuffed with clothes, toys, games and books. Perched on top of it all sat the two sewing-machines, as well as our swing for Rubio to hang in a tree in the garden.

The so-called 'châlet' was a large, battered old house, built on no intelligible plan. Even in summer, as we soon found out, it was damp and dark as a dungeon. Trees grew through the windows, invading the rooms, and any light that might have trickled in was kept out by the curtain of creepers that swarmed all over the building. The entire house was plunged into the kind of gloom which usually obscures the bottom of an aquarium.

A long stone passage led to the only loo, which seemed a terrible bore at first, but this distance soon revealed itself as a blessing in disguise as the days passed and the time approached for the visit of M. le Vidangeur. When he finally arrived, driving his stinking, creaking lorry through the garden, and inserted a pump into a square of cement behind the house, we fled out of the front door with cries of protest.

The garden, mysterious and creepy, was full of narrow tunnels between overgrown box hedges and old cedars with huge branches snaking along the ground, all of it so tangled with vines and ivy that it could have been abandoned for a hundred years. The overall atmosphere was one of languor and melancholy decay. All this luxuriant vegetation would at least, I thought, shelter an abundant insect life, which would surely keep Marie happy for the rest of the holidays. But her first preoccupation was cleaning out the cupboards, which were lined all over with mould and mildew. After a stormy week of scrubbing and scouring every corner of the house, it took her a long time to unpack and store away all our clutter. During this cheerless period we kept well out of her way, spending most of our time in the garden.

A wall seven or eight feet high separated us from the garden next door, which sloped down to the beach. From the top of the wall it was literally child's play to swing into the cedars, and from there to proceed all the way round the garden, cruising along the treetops, creeping from branch to branch in the lime-green twilight like a troop of monkeys. Completely invisible from the ground, we took care to keep absolutely quiet, as our treetop life was like another world, a glorious in-between state, subject neither to the rigours of earthly discipline nor to the ascetic standards of heaven. Sometimes Marie would stamp about below, calling and searching, with the broad brim of her hat flapping up and down in mounting irritation.

One day we decided to build our own house in one of the tallest trees, and become established denizens of these upper regions. It took us ages to haul the boards up and nail them down into a firm platform – which in the end was about all the construction there was. Sometimes we tied a ground-sheet to the branches above, but we so much preferred to see the sky through the leaves that we soon gave up this makeshift roof altogether. All the time not spent on the beach we spent in our tree-house. So far we had managed to get up there unseen, until one day Christine, who was about 2 at the time, caught us at it. 'Me want to go up too,' she announced. We explained why this was impossible. She insisted, and we told her to run away and play. She let out a piercing scream. 'Me going to tell Marie,' she yelled. The little pest was going to sneak, and that would be the end of our treetop life.

I slithered to the ground and ran to the woodshed to collect a basket, into which she squeezed. Then, tying a rope to the handle, I scrabbled up again with the rope in my teeth. We started to haul her up. All went well until the basket began to swing and crashed into the tree. Christine let out an ear-splitting screech. As the rope grew shorter, the whole arrangement began to spin. 'Going to be sick,' she wailed. 'Shut up,' ordered John, 'or we'll drop you.' Soon she was jammed beneath the floor-boards, and the harder we pulled the more we flattened the poor creature into her basket. 'We've got to get her *over* the edge,' I kept saying. 'We can't pull her *through* the floor . . .'

In the end, as she came into view on a forward swing, we whipped her over the edge with a swift manoeuvre. When we finally got her out of her basket she was white-faced and quivering like a jelly. I sat her on my lap and calmed her down while John tied the rope around her waist, with the other end firmly tethered to a branch. 'If you fall overboard we can yank you back,' he told her. 'But try not to all the same.'

After that episode we took good care to shin up our tree only when we knew that Christine was well out of range.

On very hot days, Marie, who hated the sand, the sun and the sea, marched us off to the forest behind the sand dunes. There she would settle under some vast oozing pine, which spewed resin from every pore: its fumes, inhaled into our tubes, would, she believed, keep off winter colds and wheezes. In Vence she frequently made us play in the shade of eucalyptus trees for the same reason. And there she sat, happily knitting away our endless winter socks, clicking and flashing her four steel needles at an incredible rate, while we mooned around, bored to death and longing for the beach. If we were lucky enough to have settled down by an ants' nest, all was well and the day was saved. Another powerful attraction were the caterpillar processions, in which thousands of them crawled along nose-to-tail in single file. Marie would even put her knitting aside for these and go down on hands and knees, peering sideways at the creatures which humped along in total unconcern. Occasionally she fished out one of her specimen bottles and scooped up a handful to take home for pickling purposes.

* * *

Owing to her regrettable thumb-sucking habit, Anne's second batch of teeth, which had lately appeared, were beginning to poke forward in an alarming way. Quite unintentionally, she was starting to damage people with them, for they were razor-sharp. From time to time you would hear John growling, 'Do be careful, you've hit me with your teeth again.'

'I can't help it,' she would wail, 'they stick out too far.'

'Well, keep your mouth shut, then.'

'I can't, my lips won't meet. It's not my fault.' And she would burst into tears.

In the end my mother took the matter in hand. As there was no dentist in St Georges, they had to go to Royan to find one. And in due course Anne was fitted out with a curious-looking object made of bakelite. This consisted of two sections which could be eased apart gradually, which was supposed to widen the roof of her mouth. It became known, not surprisingly, as 'Anne's cleft-palate'. Since she couldn't speak through it, she had to spit it out whenever she wanted to utter. Half the time, of course, the wretched thing was found lying around in the most unlikely places. John was heard to say at lunch one day, 'For goodness sake, take this ghastly thing away,' as it turned up in his table-napkin. I once found it in my pencil-box. Poor Anne's life was unmitigated misery during those cleft-palate years. On one occasion, as we were all sitting down to lunch, a loud crunching sound was suddenly heard under the table. 'Who's given Sam a bone?' asked Mamma sternly. 'You know you mustn't feed him at meals.' As we were eating skate and black butter at the time, we could claim, quite truthfully, that nobody had given Sam a bone. 'He's probably scratched one out of his store in the garden,' suggested John.

Peering under the table, we bent down in unison to remonstrate with him. Sam glared at us all in turn, and suddenly Anne wailed, 'He's got my palate!'

'Really!' exploded Mamma, 'this is too much! Why on earth did you give it to him?'

'I didn't give it to him,' whimpered Anne. 'He must have pinched it out of my pocket.'

'Well, get it back at once. I've never heard of such a thing.'

As Anne went down on her knees under the table, Sam uttered a deep growl of warning. 'He likes it,' remarked John. 'He's never had anything so tasty before.'

'Don't be so disgusting,' said my mother. 'And be careful, Anne, he might bite . . .'

'Of course he won't bite,' I said indignantly. 'Sam never bites!'

Anne crept forward another inch, and Sam's lips curled back in a snarl as his hackles rose. They glared at each other, eyeball to eyeball. This seemed likely to go on forever. Suddenly my nerve broke and I was shaken by a violent sneeze. Sam gave a start, and Anne pounced on her palate. 'I've got it,' she yelled in triumph, reappearing at table level. 'Well, go and disinfect it at once,' ordered Mamma. 'Ask Marie for some of her pickling spirits, and make sure it's completely clean.' When we next saw the object, it was floating in a jam-jar full of spirits, between a pickled snake and a four-legged chicken on the top shelf of the kitchen dresser. And after a suitable length of time it was duly returned to poor Anne's mouth.

13

In spite of the damp, the darkness and the persistent smell of mildew in the house, our first summer in St Georges was pure bliss. For three long hot months we lived on a beach of white sand three miles long. We paddled and shrimped and 'swam' in the shallows with one foot on the bottom, and so gentle were the waves that we never had to wear life-belts (rubber rings, water-wings and suchlike were still inventions of the future at that time).

The only fly in the ointment was the daily gym lesson, on which my mother insisted, to 'keep us in shape', whatever that might mean. So every morning after breakfast we trotted down to the beach where the PT instructor, M. Dupont, marshalled us and other reluctant children from the surrounding villas into lines and columns like a battalion in training. Running, jumping, skipping, hand-stands – whatever he did in front of us we had to copy. For a solid hour, in the full heat of the sun, he marched us about, forming squares, circles, stars and set-pieces with other children standing on top of us, digging their toe-nails into our shoulders, or balanced on their heads resting their feet on our chins.

At the end of the lesson he chased us all into the sea, to pick out those who sank from the ones who could swim. He left the latter to their own devices, then pulled out the sinkers and flung them on the beach. As we were among this lot, he cornered Mamma and persuaded her that we would all drown before the end of the summer unless he taught us to swim. And from then on this was one more ordeal we had to face every day after gym.

Following lunch, for which we returned to our sombre villa, came the siesta on the beach. Mamma made us lie flat on our backs, stripped to the waist, and popping seaweed on to our chests, she rubbed the slimy jelly into the skin. This, as everybody knew, being full of iodine and other precious minerals, would be baked into the bloodstream by the sun, thus keeping coughs and colds and wheezy chests away for the whole winter. Then, when done on one side, we were turned over for basting and roasting on the other. How she managed to keep up this boring performance for a whole summer I cannot imagine. But I suppose her reward came the following winter when we caught nothing worse than measles – plus a dose of pneumonia for myself.

Moved by one of her sudden flashes of inspiration, on which she always acted without a second's hesitation or reflection, Mamma had decided to bring us to St Georges because it was home to her friends Pierre and Camille Darlange, whom she had known in Malaya when she met and married my father in 1920. Their own son Jacques had been born a few months before I arrived on the scene. We had often been trundled together in the same pram under the garden banana trees at Assam Java, and presumably had also received a bedtime whiff of chloroform from the same bottle.

When Pierre and Camille left Malaya for good, they went to live in Paris, but they always spent the school holidays at Pierre's family home in St Georges, where his parents had lived since time immemorial. Nostram was a very large old village house, in which Pierre's five brothers and sisters, and all their children, gathered for the summer holidays, and often Christmas and Easter as well. Jacques now had two sisters, Ninette and Nadia, not to mention innumerable cousins. To have friends we could meet freely on the beach, as it were on neutral ground, at any time, was a new, exhilarating experience. We became inseparable, like a shoal of fish, all moving instinctively in the same direction. And when we had to part for meals, and go home at night, it was just as painful as it is for lovers.

The Darlange children, built on a large scale, were twice as big as we were, and I suspect that our mother, secretly envious of her friends' brood of giants, submitted us to those daily gym lessons on the beach in an effort to stretch us upwards and outwards as much as possible. But I regret to say that although we were put through this infinitely dreary performance for many years, she was defeated in her purpose and we remained just as we were, growing at our own leisurely pace, and as thin as stick insects. We felt agonizingly self-conscious as we were put through our paces day after day, watched by our friends, who sat among the dunes patiently waiting for us.

When we tired of bathing and building sand-castles, we scrambled over the reef which was left uncovered at low tide.

Thickly carpeted with bladder-wrack, it was very slippery and we were continually cutting open our elbows and knees. Even more exciting were the discoveries we made as we jumped from rock to rock exploring the pools left behind by the retreating tide, which were filled with water life of every kind, from sea spiders to prawns and baby squid.

Right on the edge of the reef close to the sea was a very large pool, where flying squid flicked their way from end to end until finally swept away when the tide came in. Supposed to be quite brainless, these extraordinary creatures are said to have hearts as strong as a power-station. Whelks glided through the seaweed, curling around any shell they came across and sawing away at it with their long, knife-like tongues, edged all round with hundreds of razor-sharp teeth growing in rows of three. As soon as one set snapped off, another rushed forward to take its place. With this equipment, they had no trouble at all boring through the toughest shells and sucking the unhappy molluscs out.

The sea anemone, for all its eyeless, mindless state, is organized beyond belief. From time to time one of them will suddenly split asunder, each half quickly growing into a new, fully fledged anemone. Should any scraps fall off during the split, these will grow at once into minute members of the expanding family. Nothing is wasted. At other times they go broody and decide to lay eggs instead. And these are hatched within the folds of their own stomach pouch. How the new brood avoids being digested along with the latest meal is a mystery. But having bypassed this fate, they float away with the debris of their parents' lunch, in search of adventure on the high seas.

Starfish, the real tigers of the pools and to be found in great numbers everywhere, wriggled along on their tiny tubular feet. They have so many of these that when one set gets tired they tuck it up and let down another lot to take over. These creatures are also equipped with powerful suction pads, which come in useful for prising open clams and oyster shells determined to remain closed. The starfish will wrap its arms around the shell, switch on the suction, and use all its feet in turn until the unhappy clam or oyster, exhausted by the struggle, simply has to let go. The big bully will then shoot out its stomach, wrap it around the occupant, and digest it alive. Sea cucumbers were another intriguing group, some fat and short, others long and hollow like macaroni. I once picked up a fat one, but dropped it in a hurry as the revolting brute spat all its guts out in my face. Then away it lurched to knit itself a whole new set of insides.

Sea horses, those seductive creatures, swung about in the deeper pools as if suspended on a thread, or curled their tails around a seaweed stalk. I never saw them eating anything, although we brought them crumbs, tiny water-fleas, and any other scraps we could find. They swam up, nosed at our offerings with their little snouts, then floated away in disgust. Sea snails crawled about everywhere in profusion. We once got into trouble for collecting a jarful of them as a present for Marie. Next morning the jar was empty, and most of the snails were swarming over the sugar, the coffee-beans, the breakfast bread and croissants, while the rest were cruising along the ceiling.

At very low tide the oyster-beds on the reef were revealed. Their shells, as lethal as broken glass, slashed our gym shoes to ribbons. Cemented as they were to the rock, they seemed to lead a dull life, their sole excitement being their annual sex-change, one year male and the next female. Crowded in dense colonies, they were condemned to the company of their next-door neighbours for life, as there was no hope of moving around in search of new faces.

Our aquarium at home was a large washtub sunk into the ground in the garden, with a wire fence all round to keep out cats. Marie already had a collection of the local feline population under her wing. The aquarium was a faithful copy of the pools in the reef. We had even managed to chip off bits of rock with oysters attached, which we spread around the sides. These were covered with kelp and other weeds for the sea horses, and for the slugs and snails that snuggled in its shelter. For the whelks we brought a daily supply of clams, and for the anemones we went shrimping at low tide. The starfish gobbled up everything they came across, and the sea urchins hoovered up the sandy bottom, disposing of shrimp legs and soft crab-shells as well as any other debris lying around. After my adventure with the sea cucumber, we decided to leave that breed alone. Tiny, soft-shelled green crabs scuttled about everywhere, and we even had a baby jellyfish. But he (or she) soon disappeared, probably digested by one of the sea anemones.

A great pleasure which we enjoyed so to speak second-hand was fishing. Following the top of the cliff above our reef was a narrow path where a number of fishermen had a permanent pitch. At high tide they lowered large square nets hanging from a rope, which was wound up and down on a pulley. When the tide began to ebb, we raced to the cliff to inspect the catch of the day. The waters of the bay, nourished as they were by the village drains, sustained a rich and varied marine population. There were sole, crabs, lobsters, grey mullet, dabs and plaice, and sometimes a clutch of drowned new-born kittens. The first time we were given a batch of these by the fishermen, we flew home to resuscitate them, convinced that they were merely in a bad way. We placed them, all carefully tucked up in cotton wool, in a wooden box beside the kitchen furnace, and tried to force warm milk into their small, clamped-down mouths. On the third day, the usual day for resurrections, we lost all hope when the little creatures seemed to have shrunk still further into themselves, and Marie declared that she would not put up with these stinking cadavers in her kitchen any longer. So we were forced to bury our poor little corpses.

* * *

At the end of September the Darlange family returned to Paris, and we had to abandon our thriving aquarium when Marie suddenly told us to collect our belongings, as we were returning to Vence next day. While we were away, Fred the farmer had died, and Madame Rose, now his widow, had gone back to Switzerland. So Marie took over the kitchen for the time being.

A couple of months after our return, Papa came home on leave, and Mamma decided to do away with the little farmhouse and its stables. Her latest scheme was to remodel it as a 'winter residence', much smaller and warmer, and easier to run than Mas Mistral. And when it was finished, furnished and fit to live in, they called it Esterel, after the mountain it overlooked in the west, the kingdom of the local fairy, Esterelle. The local priest came up from the village to perform the blessing rites, leading us all in solemn procession over the whole house, sprinkling holy water in every corner to drive out the devil and his minions.

As the distance between the two houses was only about 150 yards, the move was simply a matter of running back and forth with piles of clothes, books, silver, bedding and kitchen equipment. When the time for the move finally came, we spent the rest of the week staggering up and down the path like pack-mules, dumping our loads in the new kitchen where Marie was floundering about trying to bring some order to the monumental muddle.

When everything was more or less sorted out and in its rightful place, Mamma once more remembered our education. The word 'governess' began to crop up from time to time in her conversation, and we all shuddered, but fortunately for the time being it remained no more than an idea. Meanwhile, one day in late autumn, an appalling storm suddenly struck.

Mamma and I were curled up in our chairs in the drawing-room, engrossed in our books and only vaguely aware of the tempest raging overhead. With our feet tucked up on account of the draughts, we were oblivious to what was going on around us, until a rug began to float on the water seeping, then swirling, into the room.

Perhaps after this the house was damp, or the thought of a new governess was haunting me. Shortly afterwards I went down with pneumonia. Cupping and hot mustard poultices having done no good, I lay on my bed, shaking and panting for breath, with tears rolling down my face at the pain in my side. Marie came in every two hours to wrap me from head to foot in a soaking, ice-cold sheet to bring down my temperature. And as she spun me over, tightening the sheet around me, she growled at my tears and groans and told me to stop behaving like a baby. Her philosophy was never to sympathize, as it only made you feel sorrier for yourself. And I think she may have been right.

I was lucky compared to the peasant children of my generation. They had to put up with far worse remedies, such as swallowing the juice of crushed live snails mixed with sugar, or having a pigeon split in half and clamped, still palpitating, to their heads, or freshly torn-off rabbit skins wrapped round their chests. Worst of all, they continually had to suffer the most dreadful indignities connected with their nether regions. Little pellets of soap or cloves of garlic were pushed up their bottoms and, most astonishing of all, constipation was treated with the insertion of a violet. What happened when violets were out of season leaves one wondering. Whooping cough, when it resisted snail juice, was cured by pushing the child seven times backwards and forwards under the belly of a donkey. Some of these animals were famous for miles around for their curative powers, and the patients were driven to far-distant villages for their treatment, bumping along the mountain paths in horse-carts. But in spite of all this care and trouble, child mortality was very high.

After what seemed like weeks of painful illness and even more painful treatment, I began to pull through and gradually feel better. One glorious morning Papa came and sat beside me with a book. This unexpected treat made up for everything. He read me the *Divine Comedy* from beginning to end. And I remember thinking how lucky I was that it was in French and not Italian. It was pure bliss to lie back in bed, with a large pipless orange in my hands (something quite new at the time), listening to his dear weak voice while gazing out of the window at the pale spring sky and the olive trees waving slowly from side to side.

When we had squeezed everything we could out of Dante, Papa read me extracts from a huge tome of Rabelais' complete works, and we both rocked with laughter at the adventures of Pantagruel, Panurge and Gargantua. Papa was in one of his rare frivolous moods, reading the sixteenth-century French with the local *accent du pays*, which made it sound even funnier. Then he read Lamb's *Essays of Elia* in English, and the mood changed to one of delicate melancholy. Soon after this I got up and went downstairs, feeling weak and light-headed, and Papa once more withdrew into himself and his study. From then on, he hardly seemed even to recognize me when we met in the hall or on the stairs.

All this time John and Anne had been leading a busy and engrossing life *à deux* in the garden, and they didn't want me either. Though we normally spent most of our time together, we still had our own private occupations which we kept quite secret, and when one of us went off with a determined step and a certain air, the others kept away and asked no questions. And so I never knew what they were up to when John pottered about with a busy look on his face or Anne wandered away vaguely with two hats on her head.

My own favourite private occupation demanded a great deal of concentration and was a thoroughly satisfying experience. It consisted of sitting in the fork of a mimosa tree in bloom, and trying to *feel like the tree*. Nothing in the world seemed more delightful than having sprigs of mimosa sprouting out of your arms and legs and the tips of your fingers. It was really a question of the time available. If you were called away, or distracted too soon, nothing much happened. But when a long sunny afternoon stretched ahead, you could be pretty sure of plugging into the 'tree-feeling' fairly quickly. Quite soon your own identity floated away, and you became a living part of the tree itself, rippling in the breeze and tingling with the little thoughts and feelings that came rushing up out of the ground, usually so tenuous and elusive that you could never catch them any other way. But when the mimosa went out of season there was nothing more to do than moon around, sitting for hours on the swing Rubio had rigged up for us in an old olive tree, chewing pomegranates and spitting out the pips for the ants to take home to their babies.

Everything seemed out of joint. So in a way it was a relief when the new governess at last appeared. Spring set in early that year, and the move back to the big house for the summer coincided with her arrival. So her first job was to help us bundle our belongings back to Mas Mistral, and store them in their rightful places under Marie's eagle eye.

Since then I have often wondered what the new governess must have thought when she arrived, to be greeted on the doorstep by a mountain of household chattels and her new charges shooting out of the house one after the other, with armfuls of clothes, blankets and saucepans. When later she plucked up the courage to ask Marie the reason for this seasonal tidal flow backwards and forwards from one house to the other, the curt reply was that 'the children needed a change of air'.

14

Mademoiselle B, always pleasant and quite harmless, was, I think, a little bemused by the abysmal depth of our ignorance. She had probably never come across anything quite like it before, and wasn't sure how to tackle the problem. Hoping perhaps to win us over, she did away with the needle-sharp nibs and purple ink, allowing us to use pencils instead. John, being of a practical turn of mind, enjoyed doing sums, with their nice friendly adding up and different combinations of the same figures, so that he could always rely on the results. At that time he had a passion for headgear, and was never seen without something on his head. It could be an old disused work-basket or a discarded bathing-cap with a strap under the chin. But more often than not he was totally invisible beneath one of Marie's enormous garden hats. As each was far too big for him, the breeze got hold of the brim (we worked under the cherry tree on the terrace) and the whole thing rotated quite freely on his head. With his face all screwed up in concentration, and with the fingers on his left hand uncurling for counting, he was quite oblivious to the movement of the huge hat, but I, with my feeble powers of concentration, found it distinctly distracting. I never quite knew which way round it would go next, or on what side to expect the little black patent-leather bow to reappear. As for myself, I managed to convince Mlle B that my only so-called skills lay in drawing, painting, reading and writing stories. These were the only subjects I could understand or work at. To my amazement, she fell for it, and so I was able to spend all my 'lesson' time doing pictures for my stories, often before they were even written.

Anne, by fixing her enormous oyster-coloured eyes unblinkingly on our teacher, had learned the useful trick of hypnotizing Mlle B into letting her get away with doing nothing at all. There she sat, with her thumb in her mouth, steadily pushing out her front teeth, her huge eyes following Mlle B's every movement. So lessons on the whole were relaxed and uneventful, and I never learned a thing under that regime.

To encourage at least a degree of self-education, we had the freedom of my father's bookshelves, where we could read anything we liked, except for the *Larousse Médical*, a huge tome which was strictly forbidden. For extra safety it was stored out of reach on top of the highest shelf in the study, so that getting at it was a hazardous, even dangerous operation. And if we ever managed to lower it to the floor without an almighty crash, there was always Marie's ultra-sensitive radar system to be reckoned with. So our only hope hung on one of her rare visits to Nice to have her eye attended to.

Every page of this delectable book was adorned with pictures of the most appalling diseases and conditions. Many of them, as an extra bonus, were in colour. I remember gruesome tumours, like Californian sunsets, ears that really *looked* like cauliflowers, strawberry noses, some without nostrils, and Siamese twins glued together at various points in their anatomy. There was one really sickening case of elephantiasis, in which the patient's penis had grown all the way down to his feet and looked for all the world like a third leg. And I remember looking at John with my heart all twisted with pity at the thought that on account of his sex he too, poor boy, might end up stumping around in this condition one day.

But summer and winter, whether we were going through a period of education or idleness, the afternoons were always free to feed our animals and tend our own gardens and our private graveyard. It was there that we buried our dead friends, domestic and otherwise. Tastefully laid out, with gravel paths and mini-tombstones, it followed the same pattern as the village cemetery where Grandpapa was buried. It contained a great number of birds, several large lizards, two cats, a tortoise bitten through to the heart by a dog, and a porcupine.

These activities kept us going until tea-time, after which we would return to the nursery for drawing, painting and Marie's reading sessions. There was at that time an exciting new mania for flying – the kind in which you had to lean over the side of your plane to see where you were going, counting the steeples as you went, to make sure of landing in the right field. Turned into a mystical experience by St Exupéry, that high-priest of the air, it became a cult, and no one was immune to the craze, least of all ourselves. We throbbed along fervently, with Marie leading the way, when Charles Lindbergh crossed the Atlantic in thirty-three and a half hours in a 200-horsepower monoplane. She read us the books of St Exupéry, and although a lot of it was above our heads, her own suppressed excitement created an unforgettable impression.

Special leather coats were devised for pilots, for keeping out the terrible cold in the windy heights of the sky. Mamma, reacting in her own individual manner and never giving a damn for other people's reactions, acquired one of these garments, so sensible as a protection against the icy blasts of the mistral. It was a great thrill when we saw her rigged up in it, with the addition of one of her more fetching cloche hats and a stout pair of golfing shoes. Thus attired, she would set out to do her shopping, visit her friends or sort out her lawyer, the village priest or the mayor. And she always got her way.

* * *

At about this time, a couple of English ladies, Helen Hill and Violet Maxwell, rented rooms in the old farmhouse. They wrote books about the South of France and the local peasants, involving a good deal of regional history. Miss Maxwell wrote the stories and her friend drew the pictures. By then Mlle B had moved on to a more rewarding job. And before my mother had time to find a successor, Miss Maxwell came to the rescue.

She had a sweet lined white face, and seemed infinitely old (she must have been about 40 at the time). Her short, stiff grey hair stuck out like straw on either side of her cheeks. She invited us to tea under the fig trees by the pond, and over the bread and butter and cherry jam, she started to tell us the history of Vence – and it was not till much later that I realized we were having *a lesson!* After tea we had to go and write it all down – in English. This took some doing, as my spelling was still largely phonetic, and all kinds of foreign words from early childhood kept cropping up. In the end, my essays, if they could be called that, were sprinkled with bits of Provençal, Malay, Italian or just plain patois. Miss Maxwell never turned a hair. She simply remarked, 'I think the English word you want here is probably this, or that,' or whatever seemed most likely. And where the story was concerned, she would just say, 'Actually it was the Saracen invaders who were the pirates, not the Knights Templar. *They* were trying to defend the coast . . .' And with all the barbarian invasions throughout the centuries, poor Provence had certainly had more than her share to cope with.

June was now back in all its glory. The animal and vegetable life of the garden was heaving and bustling with activity. The nightingale had begun to sing in the cherry tree, and Miss Maxwell declared that nobody should be allowed to grow up without sleeping at least one night out of doors at this time of year. My mother had no objection, but there was serious opposition from Marie, who said that the night dew would seep into our bones and set up rheumatism which would stay with us for life.

As an early heatwave made the grass steam by day and the stars quiver through the heat haze at night, her arguments were unconvincing. Little Miss Maxwell, brave as a lion, carried the day, and sent us up to the attic to collect hammocks. Strung up in the fig trees by the pond, our bedding dangled over the animal graveyard. Taking care to avoid the tiny tombstones, Miss Maxwell tucked us up in our rugs and left us to experience our first night out of doors. Listening intently to the noises of the night, we were so excited we could hardly breathe. The deafening sound of the cicadas gradually died, and the field crickets set up their plaintive dirge. Then suddenly, sharp as a knife, came the first notes of the nightingale. He tried out a few trills at first, then, finding his voice, got going in earnest. On and on he went, gaining confidence, changing the odd note here and there, then settling down to a truly magical performance.

Pungent smells began to rise from the ground. A field mouse squeaked, and fireflies flickered among the fig leaves, taking their time, each allegedly searching for a wife but in no great hurry to find one. From time to time a fig plopped into the pond or a goldfish leaped at a firefly, while above our heads the dark-blue sky displayed its myriad stars. Squelchy thumb-sucking noises coming from Anne's hammock announced that she had dropped off. But John and I stayed awake a long time, entranced by the revelations of the hot June night.

It was still pitch-dark overhead, though a mustard-tinted light edged the horizon over the sea, when we were woken up by the hysterical chatter of the birds. This was the first time I realized that birds tune up *before* sunrise, and by the time the sky turned milky at the approach of dawn, they had switched off their chorus and gone dead quiet. For about fifteen minutes, a strange new warmth puffed up all around, while not a sound was heard. The world seemed wrapped in cotton wool. Then gradually the air freshened as the sky grew lighter, and twigs and leaves began to rustle as insects got on the move. Not until the sun was well up did the birds begin to sing again. But this time it was in a quick and chatty way, as they hopped about their business, clearing out their nests and bustling around for grubs.

When Miss Maxwell came round a little later, she listened to our excited comments in silence but offered none of her own in exchange. And later that day she made us write it all down, so we should never forget the experience of that wonderful night.

All through the war I followed the army around the Mediterranean theatre of war with Hill and Maxwell's little books on Vence until they, along with all my gear, disappeared during the Italian campaign. But that is another story.

* * *

Since our return from Malaya I had been regularly visiting Mrs Hillier's kitchen and nursery, and this helped to keep my English going; it would have completely withered otherwise. In another effort to keep it up, Mamma took us to an English children's 'club' in Vence run by 'Auntie', on the first floor of her tea-room on the Place du Peyra. There we played Happy Families, Hunt the Slipper, Postman's Knock and Hide and Seek.

Auntie was a middle-aged English spinster who had lived in Vence since time immemorial and befriended painters and writers. Norman Douglas always stayed with her on his way through (presumably to and from Capri), and after D. H. Lawrence had come to die at the Villa Robermond next door to Mas Mistral, Auntie rooted out his gravestone and stored it under her kitchen sink for safe-keeping. It was always fascinating to slip away from playing Happy Families upstairs and sneak into the tea-room on the ground floor to listen to the grown-ups' chatter.

Auntie, who always insisted on speaking her atrocious French to my mother (who invariably answered in her equally atrocious English – but as neither listened to the other it didn't matter in the slightest and everyone was perfectly happy), returned from Nice one day after an appendix operation, firmly convinced that a pair of forceps had been left inside her. She could feel them rattling, she declared, as she shuffled around her tea-room. And insisting on being opened up again, she was proved right, and the instrument, which she proudly kept under a glass dome, was always produced for her guests' inspection.

Vegetarians and nudists ('cranks', as we called them) frequently dropped in for tea and toasted buns, and we sometimes came across their camps during our country walks. Given to beards and sandals and fringed garments (when they wore anything at all), they were the forerunners of today's hippy communes. One of them, whom we called 'Jesus Christ', was a great favourite of ours. Gentle and harmless, he drifted about the streets in long flowing robes, with curly hair and beard, looking noble and prophetic, a character straight out of the Bible.

We often met the stage-designer Gordon Craig, swinging along in his black cloak and hat, and he and Papa politely bowed to each other, while a civil exchange of 'Morning Craig, Morning Fesq' passed between them. But as far as I know, the friendship went no further. Matisse, who lived on the Route de St Jeannet, hardly ever left his house, whereas Chagall was often seen prowling around the market stalls.

Another character who also flourished at that time, and staggered about the streets of Vence carting buckets of raw, bleeding meat, was a wild-looking woman who lived in a large house in which she harboured five or six dozen cats. Her downtrodden husband was miserably eking out the last days of his life under the same roof in total neglect. His wife and her trusty serving wench crouched all day long over the kitchen fire with a bottle of wine between them, while the cats spat and hissed at one another over the buckets of meat, and the wretched husband lay dying in his soiled, unchanged sheets. The cats, which he feared and hated, spent long busy nights with him, conducting passionate love affairs, fighting one another to the death, and leaving their messes all over his bed.

At the end of the war when, after a long and protracted agony, the poor man was eventually hustled out of this world with the cats' assistance, his wife packed up all their mutual belongings and trundled them up to Mas Mistral, to be stored in the attic for safe-keeping. Why my mother, in the unthinking kindness of her heart, permitted this is hard to tell, but Anne's husband, who was there at the time and was press-ganged into helping with the operation, told me recently that even the largest pieces of furniture were heaved up the attic stairs.

The poor woman was eventually taken off to an asylum when her behaviour, even by Vence standards, became too eccentric. Before that I often passed her sitting on a stone at her garden gate, upbraiding her geraniums in reproachful tones.

15

The happy arrangement with Miss Maxwell and her afternoon 'tea-lessons' under the fig trees was not to last. It was the village priest who ruined it all one day when he tackled my mother about our education. I think our impending confirmation was the reason for his presence at lunch that day. Mamma, who was on generally good terms with the Church, did occasionally tell the priest how to run his business. This time the roles were reversed.

'Well, my girl,' he said, turning to me. 'And what class are you in now?'

'We don't have classes,' I explained. 'We used to, but it's a kind of holiday.'

'Indeed,' said the priest with interest. 'Other children aren't on holiday at the moment, as far as I know.'

'Their governess has left, and I haven't found another one yet,' said my mother placidly. 'Do have a little more stew, Curé,' she added, eyeing his hollow cheeks and stringy neck. Everybody knew that parish priests lived on the breadline.

Gratefully holding out his plate, he returned to the subject. 'But why do they need a governess?' he asked.

'Well,' said Mamma, 'they must have some sort of education. Mind you, they can read and write,' she added hastily.

'What about the village school? What's wrong with that?'

'The *village* school?' Mamma looked startled. That was one thing she hadn't thought of. Why indeed *not* the village school? Always open-minded, she was quite prepared to consider this possibility.

And so it came to pass that in the autumn we were enrolled at the École Communale, on the far side of the village. Mamma, determined to do the thing properly, took a long searching look at the other children to see how they were turned out, and a few days later we were rigged out as little peasants, with wooden-soled lace-up boots and rough-haired navy cloaks reaching down to the ankle. These bulky garments, so useful to shepherds high up in the icy mountain passes of the Alps, were much too hot and heavy on balmy days. And in a raging wind, when the mistral was roaring down the railway cutting, our cloaks would lift high in the air as we crossed the railway bridge, and come crashing down over our heads, sometimes actually knocking us off our feet.

As it turned out, school was not as bad as we had expected. Although we were forty-strong in my class, silence and order reigned throughout the lessons. The classroom windows had been nailed shut for the winter, and the coal stove, red hot and roaring steadily, belched out its fumes all day long. Those who had been sewn into their clothes for the winter itched and scratched a good deal as the heat of the room increased, and on wet days the air was filled with the stifling smell of steaming child.

We were split into two sections, the dumb and the not so

dumb. I was in the first category. The teacher promised to move us up to the higher level as soon as we proved capable. I decided to concentrate on literature, the Greek and Roman civilizations, history and geography. Maths and algebra I found totally incomprehensible.

To begin with, following Mamma's decision that we would conform in every way, we had lunch in the canteen, where soup, the only course, was dished up in army mess tins together with half a loaf of bread. The boys, whose playground was on the other side of the wall, joined us for lunch, but we were forbidden to talk to them. John, whenever I caught sight of him, looked so gloomy that it made me want to cry. But Anne seemed to have found her feet, and was the centre of an animated group obviously hanging on her every word. I often wondered what stories she was telling them.

We never knew what went wrong with this arrangement, but it soon came to an end. From then on we were each given a packed lunch and forbidden by Marie to go near the canteen. As the classrooms were locked up during the lunch-hour, we had to sit in the cold, dusty, windswept schoolyard, disconsolately munching our sandwiches. I am quite sure that none of us complained about the soup, as we were quite used to taking things in our stride and accepting discomfort when it seemed inevitable.

Without explanation, this rather joyless period suddenly came to an end. We were simply told one day that we wouldn't be going to school any more. Intoxicated with our restored freedom, we galloped up and down the garden, yelling our lungs out and rolling down the sloping banks. After a couple of days we sobered up and returned to our private occupations, so boringly interrupted by school. The graveyard, badly neglected, was buried in weeds. Some of the crosses had fallen down, and a quail's sepulchre had been desecrated by a cat.

When the graveyard was tidied up I went to inspect my own garden. Here all was desolation and decay. The soil was dry and cracked and all my plants had died from lack of care and water. Totally discouraged, I went off to check what was going on in the hedge which grew along the eastern boundary of the garden, where oaks, hazel and fig trees flourished undisturbed. Blackbirds, blue tits and finches ran up their annual nests there, and tree-creepers and woodpeckers had their permanent holes. I threw myself down on the grass and lay absolutely still, watching the dogged perseverance of an ant as it towed a grasshopper's wing up one side of a blade of grass and down the other, on its way to the family nest. Once again we had escaped the dreaded 'education' – for the time being at any rate – and the knowledge was pure bliss.

* * *

The following June, Mamma felt the call of the Atlantic beating in her veins again. A villa was booked in St Georges, and once more the leather trunks came thumping down the attic stairs, propelled by Rubio's rope-soled espadrilles. Papa, who was coming home on leave, would meet us in Marseilles and we would continue the journey together. We were overjoyed at the thought, and at the prospect of having him with us for three whole months.

If he was pleased to see us, he showed no sign of it. He ignored us for the entire journey, only addressing a few words in German to Marie. But, apart from giving deep and frequent sighs, rolling his eyes and tapping his breast as if in pain from time to time, he appeared to be in good spirits.

The journey to the Atlantic coast went smoothly. The midnight feast which Marie produced was up to its usual standard, nobody was sick or got trapped in the *toilettes*, and the train arrived at Royan on time. As the horse-drawn coaches now plied their trade along the seafront for tourists only, we hired a fleet of taxis and set off for St Georges.

Although just as uncomfortable as we expected, Pépé was the least smelly of our holiday villas. In the yard at the back was a companionable two-seater privy, with round windows cut out in the door for callers to peer in and see who was at home. Marie, who was once more in charge of the cooking, had to sweat over the usual furnace to make the merest cup of tea, and the whole house was shrouded in the dust of the preceding winter. We all managed to fit in somehow – an achievement, since it was much smaller than anything we had ever previously rented. Rubio was squeezed into a kitchen cupboard, while Anne, Christine and I were all squashed into a tiny bedroom. John moved in with Marie, and our parents had a room to themselves, while poor Sam whimpered the nights away in the dining-room.

We spent all our time on the beach, or at Nostram with the

Darlanges. As long as we turned up on time for meals, we were allowed the most complete and blessed freedom, apart from the morning when we had to resume gym lessons with M. Dupont. And, of course, the swimming lessons had to start again. On and on they went, until he announced we were at last ready to take the swimming test, which included the dreaded, all-important life-saving certificate.

The ordeal took place in the harbour in front of the entire population of the village, with the aid of the fire-brigade's brass-band, which blared rousing marches throughout the afternoon. The judges sat in a rowing boat at the end of our 'run', where we had to turn and swim back to the starting-point on the jetty. There had been a heavy storm the night before, and the sea was dark and murky. When we lined up on the jetty and looked down, we saw that the water was bubbling with jellyfish. With a gasp of horror I turned to M. Dupont and said we couldn't possibly swim in *that!* His answer was to push me in.

We all flopped on top of the soft yielding mush and went under, thrashing about among the jellyfish. It was like trying to swim in tapioca pudding. Within seconds their tentacles were twined around my arms, creeping round my neck and trailing across my face. Somehow or other, most of us managed to make it to the judges' boat. Those who couldn't get there had to be hooked out.

We then had to turn and start on the return journey. As we scrambled up on to the jetty, we were all pushed in again to do the life-saving part. This consisted of dragging an inert body along, making sure the head was well out of the water, as far as the judges' boat once more. Having made your mark there, you had to haul your unhappy victim all the way back to the jetty. There you handed him or her over to M. Dupont, who confirmed that the job was successfully done and the poor wretch was still alive. After that it was your own turn to take the victim's role. As my own 'saver' was in an even worse state of panic than I was, she pulled me under much more than she kept me above the surface. So that when I reached dry land at last, my mouth, full of jellyfish, felt as if I had chewed a hornets' nest.

The ordeal was over at last and we had our 'pass' badges, but we were covered with stinging weals on every inch of uncovered skin. By evening we were puffed up all over, as if blown up with a bicycle-pump, with eyelids painfully glued together. Marie, grinding her teeth in disapproval, dumped us in a boracic bath, and spent the next few hours sponging our throbbing faces.

After this, Mamma, ever anxious to improve our physique, devised a most terrible, lolloping walk for us which was designed to arch the feet, loosen the joints and tone the muscles all in one go. It was, according to her, the best possible exercise for developing young growing bodies, so two or three times a week we were led off to the pine woods along the beach. This conferred a double benefit, as we would be breathing in all those valuable essences at the same time.

Completely unselfconscious as she was, our mother broke into her lollop, enjoining us to do the same, before we had even left the village. John and Anne followed her, doubled-up with laughter, while I hobbled behind with tears of shame and humiliation running down my face, as people stopped, stared, and exclaimed: 'Oh, poor things, do look! Whatever is the matter with them?' We looked like a family all cursed with the same strange affliction. Curiously, Mamma minded the laughter much less than the tears, which she said I produced on purpose to draw attention to myself and make people feel sorry for me. And so we lolloped along, rocking from heel to toe, flexing the knees, flinging out the arms ('From the *shoulder*, I tell you! Those feeble little wiggles are no good at all!') and thrusting out the hip-joints this way and that like a group of belly-dancers. When this performance was over, and we had hobbled disjointedly back to Pépé, we rushed to the beach as fast as we could, in case Mamma should think up some new form of body-building exercise for us.

It was a great joy to be able to swim really well at last. No breaker, however huge, was frightening any longer. We dived straight through them, gliding in the glassy water, and learnt how far we could go before coming up for air. Twice a year, at the time of the equinox, the tide went out much further than usual, and the sea withdrew for miles. The harbour was drained to the dregs, exposing all the treasures on its bottom: old prams, cartwheels, toy boats, broken bidets, and so on. The firm wet sand came to an abrupt end, and the primeval oceanic mudflats stretched away in the distance, bubbling and wriggling with their own private life. Lugworms, like strips of raw liver, dived head down into the slime. Razor shells peered out of their holes, tiny green crabs scrambled frantically into the mud, and all kinds of nameless, shapeless blobs of jelly wriggled about, waiting for the sea to return. And all this snapped, crackled and popped as millions of tiny bubbles erupted everywhere.

The first time we saw the tide go out so far we ran along the edge, breathing in the deep rich smell which came wafting out of the ooze. Suddenly, overcome by an irresistible urge, I threw myself flat on my face in the mud. John and Anne followed instantly, and we rolled about, slapping and whacking the slimy surface with flailing arms, unconsciously reaching back millions of years to our original home in the warm Cambrian seas, where our ancestors, all those bits of quivering jelly, first came to life. Black and dripping from head to foot, we jumped back on to solid sand and raced home to show Marie, who we knew would be fascinated by the look and feel of this extraordinary substance so seldom seen.

'What do you think of this?' John asked her as the three of us, still black from head to foot, burst into the kitchen, stinking and dripping all over the floor. She ran a finger down his arm and rubbed it on the palm of her hand. 'Good, rich stuff this,' she said, 'very fertile. There's nothing to beat it. I'll get Rubio to fetch a few pails of it for the garden.' Then she hissed fiercely: 'Get back to the beach at once and wash all that filth off in the sea. And don't let me see you again before dinner.'

* * *

When the tide was rising, ah, that was when our spirits soared, and a strange new elation took possession of us all. This reaction to the advancing tide seemed to hit everybody along the beach like an electric current. And the higher the tide, the more delighted we all were. On very special occasions, freak waves even swamped the beach tents and carried away bits of underwear and other belongings, and we dived in like retrievers to restore their sodden property to the distracted owners. It was then that the *plongeoir*, a high wooden structure planted in the sand and used for diving when the tide was high, came into its own. Now that we were expert swimmers we enjoyed plunging into the swell and swimming underwater, among the fish which wriggled through our hair and our hands, and nosed into our ears.

It was so absorbing that we didn't always notice when the tide was going out. On one of these occasions, I dived from the very top and landed on my head on the sandy bottom. Had it been stones I would have broken my neck. As it was, my backbone merely slipped out of joint. But this was bad enough to keep me flat on my back for the rest of the summer. Plunged into despair, I think I would have died of boredom and frustration had Jacques not come every day to sit by my bed for hours, reading aloud and playing rummy, Hangman's Noose and Battleships. He came straight from the beach, smelling of seaweed and dripping sand. My gratitude for all those hours of swimming that he ungrudgingly sacrificed to sit with me and keep up my morale, was unbounded, and my devotion and admiration for him grew as the days went by, and still he came, patient and forbearing, while the others simply put their heads round the door to say hullo and were gone. So that by the end of the summer I was totally, unquestioningly in love with him, as a dog is in love with its master.

Soon I was allowed to sit up in bed for a few days, and then to stand up and come downstairs. But there was no more swimming that year.

At about this time my mother had another of those inspirations which could turn each day into a nightmare. The high tides of the autumn equinox, withdrawing miles out into the bay, revealed the largest oyster beds imaginable, clinging to a vast shelf of rock usually hidden by the sea. Mamma spotted them at once, and day after day during the *grandes marais* she sent Rubio hotfoot with a sack and hammer and chisel to collect as many as he could before the tide turned and swept him out to sea. So each day he came home with his sack heavily laden with oysters as big as Marie's gardening shoes.

Apart from me, the entire family was delighted with these oysters, which they consumed by the dozen. But for me it was torture. The mere sight of the obscene creatures glistening in their shells made my insides heave. If I could manage to get the first one down, all was well and I bolted the rest with my eyes closed. But the minute you stuck a fork into them, they wriggled and squirmed and I would rush out of the room with my napkin over my face, howling, 'You don't realize, they've even got *kidneys!*'

* * *

John was, on the whole, a calm and placid person, wise beyond his years. When people approached him with their problems, as they often did, his advice was always judicious and succinct. But once in a while the devil got into him, and when that happened it was best to keep as far away from him as possible.

By the autumn I was fit again, and on one never-to-be-forgotten day we all set off to the forest to collect wood for Marie's furnace. We had our rucksacks on our backs and Rubio, armed with a hatchet, was harnessed to a little two-wheeled trailer. The weather was lovely and we skipped along in high spirits. Even Sam, who was getting on in years, trotted briskly along the sandy path. When we reached a spot where a lot of dead trees were lying on the ground, Rubio got to work with his axe, and we helped by pulling off the prickly branches and breaking them into suitable lengths.

After half an hour or so I noticed, with a sinking heart, that John's mood was changing. He was beginning to snap the sticks with exaggerated effort, flinging out his arms so that one of us got scratched or poked in the eye every time. When he caught Anne's skirt, lifting it high on the end of a branch, and roared with laughter, she whipped round in a fury. 'I'll hit you with my teeth if you're not careful,' she threatened. Rubio, coming in for the next round, got a sharp poke in the back of the neck. He missed a stroke and went sprawling, landing on his knees with his beret over his nose. This made John hoot with laughter again and Rubio's fierce Basque temper flared. He scrambled to his feet and made straight for John with his chopper held high. I yelled at John, 'Run, for heaven's sake, *run!*'

John leapt through the trees like a goat, with an infuriated Rubio stumbling after him. But because of his weak sight (his eyeballs had once been seriously damaged by lightning during a thunderstorm) he kept tripping over stones and stumps which he couldn't see, and John got away. After that, though we all pleaded on his behalf, poor Rubio was sent back to Mas Mistral in disgrace.

* * *

During that summer, out of the blue, Mamma took me inland to Barbezieux to stay with her friends the Fauconniers. Hélène was there with her three brothers, all of them cool, detached and haughty, like highly bred hawks. François Fontaine, who was later to become Hélène's husband, was also there. He was less a bird of prey than a stag, and God knows how I looked to them! However, after a while the ice melted, and we all played noisy and rumbustious games in the garden, where there were swings and a trapeze and parallel bars. But ever-present was that strange overriding melancholy which broods over the region around Bordeaux and which pervades the novels of François Mauriac. Insidious and seductive, it is like a kind of lotus-eating, and I felt even then that it could, if allowed, soak into the bloodstream and fix in one a mood of languid melancholy for life. More than ever did I understand the desire of those full-blooded pioneers, my two great-grandfathers, to escape this cloying, enervating miasma.

Henri Fauconnier's sister Geneviève, who wrote a blissful book about her farm, *Pastorale*, and won the Prix Femina for her novel *Claude*, lived a long way out in the country. We went there one fine day, to find a scene straight out of *Le Grand Meaulnes*. The farm and its grounds had been given over to some charity event, and there were booths, merry-go-rounds and coconut shies. Children in crinolines and knickerbockers bowled hoops along the paths and raced around, laughing and shouting.

We went into a barn smelling of warm cow and hay, and there, of all unexpected things, two American ladies, who lived in a caravan in the grounds, performed a ballet to Debussy's *L'Après-midi d'un faune*. The whole thing is so nebulous and dreamlike in my memory that, much as I would like to, I can't remember anything more precise, though I do remember that there was a great deal of old-world courtesy, and Mamma was continually having her hand kissed, which she didn't seem to mind in the least.

16

In September Mamma received another flash from on high. She announced one day at breakfast that we would not be going back to Vence for the winter. Instead she would be returning to Malaya, and she would take us all with her. This was unexpected, wonderful news. We whooped with joy.

But our euphoria didn't last. Next day she told us she had changed her mind, and we would all be staying in St Georges, and off she went to see the headmaster of the college in Royan. It transpired from this interview that he would take us all, on condition that I learned Latin before the beginning of term. There were two weeks to go. Mamma confidently assured him that there was no problem, and set off at once to find me a Latin teacher. This turned out to be more difficult than she had anticipated. The local priest, the natural choice, flatly refused to teach girls.

In the end she unearthed a very ancient scholar who was spending the remainder of his days writing a history of medieval heresies in Latin. I never discovered how she persuaded him to take me. As for me, having no idea what I was in for, I was delighted by the idea of learning such an ancient, noble language and plunged in with enthusiasm. Sanskrit, I thought, would have been even better.

When I arrived for my first lesson, my new teacher greeted me in Latin, and from then on never addressed a word to me in any other language. We were confined to his study for six hours a day, while my poor confused and untutored brain reeled. By the time I was released in the evening, all I could do was stagger down to the beach for a quick swim. After that, still bemused, I returned to the villa to do my Latin homework.

When school started two weeks later, we did not, thank goodness, have to take any kind of entrance exam. A rough guess was made, and we were placed in classes suitable to our respective ages, if not our intellectual level. As it turned out, we managed, through a great deal of hard work and a certain amount of copying from our neighbours, to scrape along at the bottom of the class. Our delight at finally being in a proper school, with children of our own age, kept our spirits up, so that our low marks didn't depress us unduly.

Apart from maths, I enjoyed all the subjects, and came across some fascinating facts. In biology, for instance, I learned that the human eyelid has the only muscle in the body that makes a noise. If you shut your eyes suddenly, you can hear a click. But you have to listen carefully, as the click is very faint. On the whole we were regarded as harmless freaks by our companions, whose judgement we accepted unquestioningly. In fact, enjoying school for the first time, we lived through that term in a kind of dream, floating a good six inches above the ground.

We had to be at school, four miles away from home, at

eight in the morning. *Le petit tram* – a small, single-gauge open train with curtained sides – picked us up every morning in St Georges at 7.30 a.m. and dropped us at the college gates at ten minutes to eight. We just had time to dash through the hall and out to the sandy schoolyard to line up with our classmates. The teachers, known as *professeurs*, were all men. The boys were all addressed by their surnames, but the girls, right down to the little 8-year-olds, were always called *mademoiselle*.

Each *professeur* had his own classroom, so that we were constantly on the move from one room to another, according to the lesson coming up next. This caused an enormous amount of traffic on the stairs and in the corridors. Endless crocodiles trudged in opposite directions, with a great deal of banter and witty exchanges on the way. Little notes and *billets-doux* changed hands constantly, assignations were made, and life was very exciting. English boys become gallant at a much later age (if ever) than the French. Most of the boys in my class, though savage in their fights with one another, were gentle and considerate with girls. They carried our books, gave us sweets, and let us copy their maths homework. They chatted us up endlessly during break, with gracious compliments on the colour of our eyes and hair. The schoolyard, where a lot of this went on, was an extension of the beach beyond, shaded by umbrella pines, and the sound of the sea was always in the air.

At midday we climbed back into our little tram which was waiting for us outside the college gates, and puffed and whistled our way through the woods, back to the villa for lunch. After which, stuffed and bloated with one of Marie's ample meals, we returned to school to snooze the afternoon away in the overheated classrooms. Fortunately the *professeurs* had also had a substantial lunch, and a great deal of their morning vigour had evaporated with the fumes of their daily bottle of burgundy.

Some of the wilder boys flicked ink pellets at the ceiling with impunity, or quietly unscrewed all the bolts on the bench in front of them, so that its occupants would suddenly crash to the floor with a frightful clatter. Sometimes a stink-bomb would go off in the aisle, creating total chaos, with everybody rushing to the windows for air. The four-o'clock bell caused a stampede, with all order gone to the wind, and everybody pelted down the stairs, swinging satchels, bellowing and whooping with released high spirits.

One of the clever girls in my class took me under her wing and helped me tirelessly with homework and moral support. Day after day she encouraged me to keep going, and when I took her home to tea, she even talked wisely to my mother about my work. A year older than me, she had a club foot and a cool and perceptive brain. I remember her with affection and gratitude, and have often wondered what became of her. She should by rights have gone to teach literature at a senior girls' school. Her parents were abroad, and she and her sister shared a small house with a governess. It was a pleasant household, calm, cultured, sensible, and with all the right values. The three of them, I realized even then, were born spinsters.

Another girl in my form who could not be ignored was a little hell-cat half my size, who had all the boys in the class under her thumb. I used to watch her giving them orders to persecute me, then waiting to see what would happen. As I was totally unpractised in this kind of warfare, my only defence was to emulate animals who feign death in the face of danger. When I saw the attack coming, I simply looked as defenceless as I felt. And this was no act. What is more, it seemed to work. Even her most devoted slaves hesitated to attack such a terrified-looking creature. As they approached, I would drop a handkerchief or a ruler. One of them would pick it up with an embarrassed grunt and hand it back to me, after which they would slink away to take their punishment. And although she kept this up for a whole term, I wasn't molested once. After the holidays she either got bored with the game or found another victim, and I was left in peace.

That autumn the film star Danielle Darrieux had launched the fashion for black plastic *ciré* raincoats, and we all wore them, boys and girls alike, whatever the weather. Those black raincoats, black gumboots and black berets were the uniform without which we never dreamt of being seen, so that in a school where there was no regulation uniform, we put ourselves into one of our own free will.

* * *

That year too we started a weekly magazine, for which we soon received so many orders that we had to spend most of our time working on it. There was a children's newspaper called *Benjamin*, to whose editor we sent a copy of our first number. He gave us a glowing write-up which started the ball rolling, and the subscriptions came pouring in. This was the last thing we had expected. The wretched thing, which had been such fun to start with, got out of hand and became a nightmare. Had we been older and more experienced, we might have been able to run it on a proper businesslike basis. As it was, we wrote it all out by hand in block capitals with special ink. The master-copy was then pressed down on to a kind of solidified jelly which absorbed the print, and from this we could run off as many copies as we needed. We ran two serials, one short story, a crossword puzzle, nature notes, a fashion feature and a page of ads, which were made up to start with.

As the whole thing was copiously illustrated, it took a great deal of time to set up. And thinking of the work involved, at 50 centimes a copy it was cheap at the price. We managed to keep it going for six feverishly hard-working months, at the end of which, distracted with exhaustion, we had to give it up. Heartbroken, we wrote to our subscribers telling them that we had to stop publication as, alas, school-work had to come first. And for several weeks after that I continued to wake up at night in a cold sweat, thinking I still had to dash off a couple of chapters for the serials before breakfast. Worst of all were the crosswords – for months we were never far from a dictionary. But on the whole, in spite of the frenzy, I think we got more fun than misery out of it.

Our next craze was for bicycles. The little tram was suddenly considered cissy, only fit for toddlers and grandmas. So my mother bought us a bicycle each, and from then on, come rain or shine, we cycled to and from school every day of the week. We either took the path through the woods, where we had to cross a stream via a creaking, worm-eaten wooden plank, or else we went by the sea-road, which took longer but was magical on sunny days.

Going home after school, we often trundled our bikes on to the beach at low tide, and raced round and round on the hard wet sand, like low-flying swallows at sunset. We devised a game of bicycle polo, in which we dealt one another the most murderous blows and crashed headlong into each other's front wheels. We often had to carry our bicycles home on our backs with a wheel twisted into a figure-of-eight. That winter all our pocket-money went on repairs and 'new' second-hand parts for our battered bikes.

Another sport that we longed to practise, but could seldom afford, was sand-sailing. Small boats made of canvas, with three wheels, a mast and two enormous sails, could be hired by the hour in Royan. In a high wind these thistledown sandcraft simply flew along the beach, and you needed skill and a good deal of nerve to control them and prevent them from taking off like kites in a high wind.

17

When the Darlange family arrived for the Christmas holidays, we all set off for the woods with saws and choppers to collect the finest tree we could find. We came back with a magnificent ten-foot-high specimen which we planted in sand, in the biggest wash-tub we could find, and then set up in front of the dining-room window. As we stood around admiring it, my head, which had been aching all day, suddenly felt as if it was going to split. My throat was on fire, and my breath hissed and whistled and rattled in my chest.

'What's the matter with you?' my mother asked suspiciously. 'Nothing at all,' I wheezed, but this remark triggered a terrible fit of coughing, at which my mother took me firmly by the hand. 'Come with me,' she said, and she produced her dreaded thermometer. After that there was no argument. Off to bed I had to go. The next day I was covered with spots and my eyelids were glued together. Lying in bed all day long, unable to eat the turkey and plum pudding Marie brought me, I sobbed into my pillow with misery at missing the revels below.

To cheer me up, Jacques brought me a copy of Kipling's *The Light that Failed*, which he had been given as a Christmas present. It was the first full-length English book I had ever read. And if it hadn't been for the chickenpox, and the terrible boredom it produced, I would probably never have got through it. But it served a useful purpose in convincing me that I really could read English at last and even enjoy it.

The rest of that school year flashed by. Lessons, totally incomprehensible to begin with, were becoming easier. My Latin teacher told me that I now knew enough to keep the headmaster happy, and so our lessons could end. The poor man, who had worked even harder than me, was worn out, and longed to shed his dim-witted pupil and get back to his heresies. Our daily lessons had even included Sunday mornings after church, and for those who can take it, I recommend this kind of immersion as the best way of getting the hang of the language, its peculiar syntax, back-to-front constructions and divine rhythm. But not everybody will think it a price worth paying.

And then the spring term was over, and the Easter holidays brought the Darlanges back from Paris, and we were all in heaven once more.

On the beach, half-buried in the sand, was a black square shooting-box known as a *tonne*, which had broken away from its moorings in the marshes, floated out to sea, and subsequently been washed up by the tide. This was one of our favourite meeting-spots at the time. Crawling through the narrow shooting slit (the door was on the opposite side, buried in the sand), we huddled inside where we felt cosy, safe and quite unassailable.

The Darlange children, who seemed to have grown even

larger in the past few months, only just managed to squeeze through. It was touch and go, but they finally made it. We were growing up and the boys, whose voices were breaking, uttered the most comical squeaks, which reduced us to helpless fits of giggles. Ninette's hair had grown into beautiful glossy waves bouncing down her back, much to Nadia's disgust, as she herself was never able to produce anything more than a few fluffy tufts around her ears, in spite of all the bottles of castor oil she poured over it. Her hair, far from being her crowning glory, was her despair, the kind of wispy fuzz that grows on babies' heads.

We would talk in the shooting-box for hours, mostly about what we had done and the books we had read; we formed plans for the future, set the world to rights, and when talk dried up, we made up stories, no one being allowed more than a five-minute stretch at a time.

One day John produced, as a surprise, some pipes which he had made for us out of bamboo canes, after which he handed round the tobacco, a careful blend of Indian and China tea. We stuffed our pipes with this concoction and lit up. Within a few seconds we were coughing and spluttering as a thick cloud of smoke filled the box, kippering our eyeballs and scorching our tongues. We squeezed out and raced home, where we found Mamma anchored to her wireless. As usual at that hour, she was trying to capture the six o'clock news through the squeaks and crackles of the 'atmospherics', as Marie called them. Creeping up to her bedroom, we each took a swig of her eau-de-cologne, good strong stuff that went down like fire and obliterated all traces of the tea-smoke on our breath.

The pipe craze only lasted a week, after which we gave up smoking – all but Nadia, who progressed to Gauloises, for which, from then on, she scrimped and saved, spending every *sou* on them that she could get hold of.

At other times, as a change from the *tonne*, we went to the *palombière*, a pigeon-hide perched on top of the tallest pine tree that ever grew. The local farmers and vineyard workers used it for shooting wood pigeons, or *palombes*, which is to me one of the most beautiful words in the French language. The tree, which was as smooth and straight as a telegraph-pole, could only be climbed by placing one's feet on nails which stuck out on either side and took you all the way up to the hide in the topmost branches. These nails, mostly old and rusty, worked loose in the bark of the tree, and often came away in your hands, if they didn't snap clean off under your feet. This once happened to me as I was nearing the top, so that I was left suspended, clinging for dear life to a couple of rusty nails, with legs flailing wildly in search of some support, thirty feet above the ground. Jacques, who was just above me, vaulted on to the platform and hauled me up by the scruff of my neck.

The hide was made for two people at most, but we were seldom less than six, and it is a wonder that the worm-eaten floorboards didn't crumble under our weight. This possibility did occasionally cross our minds, but being perched up there above everything else, with a view of the whole forest and miles of coastline, with nothing above our heads but the clear blue sky streaked with flights of wild geese and duck, was so exhilarating that it was well worth taking the risk, while extra excitement was added when a high wind blew and tossed us about like a ship on a high sea.

* * *

The following term we made friends with a girl in my class called Yolande, and she joined in our bicycle-polo games with great gusto, which surprised us a good deal, as she had a mature and dignified look which disguised her inner wildness. Completely hemmed in by her family life, she lived in a small château on the hill behind Royan, a lonely, tidy, repressed life in a wing of her own, with an aquarium full of goldfish and a governess who neglected her dreadfully. The governess only appeared at meals, when she gobbled her food in a way even we found revolting, then disappeared to her room without ever offering to help with our homework.

One spring evening, after leaving Yolande to her own homework and the silent company of her goldfish, we were freewheeling downhill on our bicycles. As we had enjoyed a particularly lively game of polo the day before, my front wheel, which had a pronounced twist, scraped the mudguard with a hideous noise. The brakes had dropped off during a head-on collision, and the only way I could attempt to slow down as we approached the main street running at right angles at the bottom of the hill was by pressing my foot down on the front tyre as hard as I could. This usually worked well enough, but in this case, under the strain, the wheel flew off and bounced away into the traffic. My bicycle pitched forward and crashed on its nose, and I was hurled against a passing car, off which, to my surprise, I bounced and hit the corner of the house across the street. Luck was on my side. I landed on my hip-bone instead of my skull, but the bicycle was flattened under the wheels of the car, which drove on as if nothing had happened.

There was no point in scraping up the remains of the bicycle, and we left them there for the dustmen to collect. Dazed and shaken as I was, I could not have managed to walk the four miles back to the Villa Pépé, and John kindly gave me a lift on his luggage-rack. It was difficult to explain to Mamma the nature of the accident that had written off my bicycle but had left me without a scratch. Willing to suffer almost any amount of pain rather than go to the doctor, I did my best not to limp. She told me to go and get myself a second-hand bicycle, and to try and look after it better in future.

* * *

It was at about this time that my mother dropped another of her bombshells. Now she really was going back to Malaya, and taking Christine with her. John was to go to boarding-school in England, and I as a boarder to a convent in Paris. Marie assured me that this fate would be worse than being exiled to Devil's Island. I believed her absolutely. Anne was the only lucky one, for she would stay on at the college and live with Marie in St Georges.

From then on, each day became so precious that I can almost recall every minute, into which we packed all the fun and pleasure we could. We got up at dawn and ran down to the beach to swim, roll down the dunes, and build enormous sand fortresses, real models of the Bastille, the Tower of London and Richard the Lion-Heart's Château-Gaillard. On our way home we bought fresh rolls and croissants for breakfast, hot from the baker's oven, and these, split in half and spread with butter, we ate under the mulberry trees with mugs of café-au-lait. Then back to the beach we went.

That summer we had a craze for playing Hangman's Noose. Sprawling shoulder to shoulder in cartwheel fashion, we would scrape out a nice pitch of damp sand, flat and smooth for drawing on. Then each of us in turn would draw a line or a squiggle, until we had a gibbet, with a rope and corpse hanging from it. As with Old Maid, the idea was to avoid at any cost being last, so that all sorts of curlicues and appendages were added, nails and screws to the gibbet, twists to the rope, eyelashes to the corpse. A fierce argument arose when someone gave him earrings. Pirates and sailors sometimes wore *one* earring, but who had ever heard of two? When bored with Hangman, we played the Word Game. This consisted of writing the first and last letter, and as many dashes as were necessary to make up the word in between. You could cheat as much as you liked by changing the word in your mind, as long as the letters already written corresponded. Then sooner or later someone jumped up and ran down to the sea, and the whole pack leapt up and followed with whoops and yells and piercing screams.

One day John and Jacques locked themselves up in the garage at Nostram. We could hear them hammering and banging away inside. But they would neither let us in nor tell us what they were up to. Eventually they flung the doors open, and there on the floor lay the most elegant little white canoe you had ever seen. They had made it themselves, to John's specifications. (Later he was to build his own ocean-going yacht, which he sailed for many years in the China Seas.) In a state of high excitement we carried it down to the beach, where it rode the waves like a swan. But what was the use of only one canoe? We clamoured for more, and they went back to work. Eventually we each had our own, which we paddled in the bay from dawn to dusk.

But the greatest excitement came with the high tides, when we raced out to where the rollers began to heave out of the sea. Once there, we swung our canoes around with a violent flip of the paddle. The movement often caused us to capsize, but with luck we sometimes managed to mount a roller at the crucial moment when it was gathering speed, and then we simply flew in to shore on it – our own home-made version of surfing. Sometimes our canoes were smashed in particularly heavy seas, and we were churned around in the raging breakers, wrapped in yards of canvas and often bruised by the flaying woodwork and gashed by exposed nails. But these small accidents were of no importance when compared with the thrill and excitement of the sport. Our great ambition was to take our boats further up the coast to the Grande Côte, where for hundreds of miles the empty beaches faced the open Atlantic. Here the undertow sucked you far out to sea before washing you up again several hours later, quite drowned, unless some lucky shark had managed to catch you on the way. But we were forbidden to paddle, let alone *swim*, on that stretch of coast.

Beach picnics were another joy. Marie, remembering her early training in Australia, produced the most fantastic spreads, over which she took a great deal more trouble than with ordinary meals at the villa. Laden with baskets and followed – before his exile – by Rubio, likewise burdened with hampers and boxes of table-silver, she would settle down at the foot of the dunes, where the tamarisks provided a thin feathery shade, and under her orders Rubio spread out the cloths, the rugs and the food. There were always fresh rolls and several kinds of saucisson, cold roast pork and chicken in aspic, big fat juicy tomatoes, egg and salmon pies, and cucumber and potato salads. Then came plum tarts and meringues, and bottles of fresh lemon juice that had been dug into the sand to keep cool.

* * *

As summer progressed, we noticed a change in Jacques. He had grown moody, and for no apparent reason would suddenly snap at one of us, then go off for long walks by himself.

It was very tiresome, as it broke the perfect harmony we had all enjoyed until then. The most ridiculous things would set him off. If he suddenly came across Nadia and me giggling helplessly over a croissant which we were nibbling from both ends, or reading the same book aloud in different accents, he would fly into a rage and stamp away, banging doors. Finally one day he took me aside and gave me a lecture. It was time, he said, for me start behaving in a more grown-up way. It was all very well for Nadia to go on being a silly little girl, but I should start to become more serious-minded. I was, after all, a whole year older than her.

This put me in a painful quandary. Loving him devotedly as I did, and knowing that one day we would be married (this was assumed, as a matter of course, by everybody), I naturally wanted to keep him happy, but the thought of giving up all the fun that Nadia and I had together was more than I could bear. This developed into a feeling of guilt, and whenever she and I went off together in one of our dotty moods, I knew that I was in some way letting old cross-patch Jacques down.

Nadia always went to bed in great style; her voluptuous form was simply made for undulating between bath and bed. To ensure the maximum audience, she retired very soon after dinner and got into one of her sophisticated nightdresses, with shoulder-straps and side-splits up to the thighs. As we had never seen anything but our own long-sleeved, high-necked Vyella nightdresses, these glamorous garments of hers dazzled us. A great deal of time was spent in the bathroom, with dogs perching and sprawling everywhere and Anne, Ninette and

I sitting on the edge of the bath like a row of swallows on a telephone wire.

Our role was to admire, advise and exclaim as she puffed out those few hairs of hers, darkened her moles, sprayed herself with scent, and tried out interesting expressions in front of the mirror. When we were all satisfied that no further improvement was possible, she swept out with one of those well-practised expressions on her face, closely followed by the snuffling dogs, and we escorted her to her room. We never knew until the last minute which bedroom she would select, or which one of her young cousins would be turned out and sent off to sleep in her bed.

When a decision had been reached, Nadia would get into bed and pick up whichever book was in fashion at the time, Victor Hugo or Racine or Corneille (she was particularly scornful of these three), and she would read aloud to us in mocking tones as we sat at her feet in fits of laughter. Sometimes, when she was feeling very magnanimous, we would be invited to squeeze in with her, squealing and giggling, with all the overexcited dogs scrabbling and scratching on top of us, barking their heads off. If she happened to have chosen a four-poster there was plenty of room, but when it was a short narrow child's bed it was a tight fit, and we screeched and squirmed and giggled frenetically. Sometimes, attracted by the noise, Jacques would walk in, shoulders and eyebrows raised in outraged disapproval. He would glare at us, and stalk out growling, 'You're all quite, quite mad', and I knew that I would be in for another lecture in the morning.

Sometimes he would tackle my mother, or she him – I never knew which way round it was – but I hated their long chats, as it was perfectly obvious that they were discussing my shortcomings and that Mamma was trying to enlist his help in improving me. More lectures invariably followed these dreaded tête-à-têtes, and although I knew he was quite right, it was intensely provoking to get the same kind of pi jaw from him as from my mother. I suppose they thought it was high time for me to become a tidy, responsible and domesticated young woman. Alas, their lectures had the opposite effect. I knew I was untidy, lazy, selfish, terribly absent-minded (a great crime, this) and did not take enough trouble with my appearance – but whose fault, pray, was that, when I still wasn't allowed a looking-glass in my bedroom, and had to wash my face with scrubbing soap?

Once, a young cousin of Jacques, who had lived in the Dordogne, came to stay at Nostram for a few days, and joined in all our activities. Tall, with dark curly hair and dreamy black eyes, he wore a brown shepherd's cloak reaching down to his feet, which gave him the romantic look of a nineteenth-century poet. We all got on very well. After he left, I was surprised to get a talking-to from Jacques. 'You were flirting with him all the time,' he said. 'You shouldn't encourage him like that, you know. It isn't fair.'

I was stunned. *Had* I encouraged him? I tried to remember. We had once sat in the dunes together, chatting about school. Another time, on the way back from a long walk, a cold wind had blown up and he had taken me under his cloak with his arm around my shoulders. Was *that* encouraging him? Perhaps it was. I suppose I could have insisted on freezing all the way home instead. I probably looked guilty, as Jacques said kindly, 'Don't worry, never mind. He won't come back.' And he never did.

When Jacques was in one of his moods, the best way to revive his happy, creative self was to get out our stories and paints and start scribbling away. In a few minutes he would come and sit next to me and pick up a paint-brush. I would read out the last chapter I had written, and he would produce one illustration after another with amazing rapidity. His people and animals were so alive that they practically jumped off the page. When a chapter was finished, we reversed roles. He wrote the next instalment, while I struggled with the drawings. We were writing a long rambling story about a caveman, his hunts and fights, and finally the capture of a beautiful girl clad in a bearskin.

Sometimes we worked at Nostram, but the constant interruptions irritated Jacques beyond endurance, particularly as he knew how much I enjoyed them. One small cousin after another would burst in with a fishing-net in need of repair, a request for sticking plaster for a lacerated knee, or even an offer to help with our painting. And best of all, Nadia would occasionally pounce and drag me away to tell me some utterly fascinating secret. So on the whole, Jacques much preferred to work at our villa.

We would spread our things out on the table in the garden, and soon Marie would come out with glasses of lemon juice or cups of tea, into which he frequently dipped his paint-brush, just as often he took a swig of the paint water, without noticing the difference. When we ran out of inspiration, he would take a book out of his pocket and begin to read aloud. After the Mowgli books, which we both loved, had been read several times over, we started on Selma Lagerlof's *Nils Holgersson,* and this enchanting Nordic tale kept us under its spell for several weeks.

The summer – 'our last summer', as we called it – slowly, imperceptibly drifted into autumn. As the sun began to lose its heat we deserted the beach and began to roam the countryside, picking great baskets of blackberries and elderberries for Marie to make into jams, jellies and fools. The elderberries never seemed quite to jell, but they produced the most haunting and subtle smell while they were cooking.

As the time of my imprisonment grew closer, I did at last become more serious-minded, and detached myself from the others to join Jacques on his lonely walks. His temper improved noticeably, and he became much kinder and more patient. That was a great relief.

18

On 1 October 1935 my mother, my school trunk and I were conveyed through the streets of Paris in a taxi to my new school in the suburb of Vincennes. For the first time in our lives we children were split up and the original plans for the others were changed. Anne was packed off to a dark and gloomy dungeon in a small provincial town in the Gironde, an experience she was lucky to survive; John went to the Jesuit College at Sarlat, where he had to wear plus-fours and a peaked cap like a chauffeur; and I was sent to Sévigné, a school which promised to turn me from a wild country creature into all that a *demoiselle de bonne famille* should be. Judging from what the others told me, I was by far the luckiest of the three.

The building, an eighteenth-century château that had belonged to one of the royal mistresses, was surrounded by enormously high walls, within which was a formal garden with gravel paths bordered by evergreen shrubs and magnificent 300-year-old cedars. Beneath the gigantic cedar in the main courtyard, we were told, La Fontaine used to read his fables to the noble châtelaine before they appeared in print. But there were no flowers, indeed no colour of any kind. A harsh formality prevailed.

On arrival, we were led to the salon where the headmistress was waiting for us. Standing in the middle of the room, drawn up to her full height, she stared at us in silence as we entered. In the dress of an abbess she must have looked formidable, and even in her long black everyday gown, with its leg-of-mutton sleeves and high lace collar, she was imposing. Since the separation of Church and state, nuns in France had been forbidden to teach, so they got round this by wearing mufti. Everybody knew of the deception, but as long as appearances were kept up, and the nuns wore what they thought was 'ordinary' modern dress, the Ministry of Education allowed them to carry on without interference.

As I shook hands with the headmistress, I felt my wrist being wrenched downwards in an iron grip, and within seconds I was almost down on one knee. My mother, who had never seen me do such a thing before, stared in amazement, but she couldn't have been more surprised than I was. This was my first introduction to the perpetual round of curtseying which went on all day long throughout the school. The 'worker-nuns' curtseyed to the pupils as they handed the dishes round at meals or when we met in the corridors. We curtseyed to the teachers, and everybody bobbed to the headmistress and to Monsieur le Chanoine, who now slowly materialized from the shadows like the Cheshire Cat. He would, I was told, be hearing my weekly confession, which was compulsory.

We were then read the rules. 'Internees', as we were called, were only allowed to receive letters from their parents. All correspondence was read and censored by the head herself. If anyone was caught smuggling a letter out of the school, immediate expulsion would follow. After this we were dismissed, and a worker-nun led us to the hall where I said goodbye to my mother. The nun then took me upstairs to the dormitory, kindly saying that I could cry until the dinner-bell but that after that no further 'signs of emotion' would be allowed.

The dormitory, as vast as a warehouse, had small square windows, high up near the ceiling, which let in practically no light. There were eighty beds, each surrounded by white curtains, and at all four corners of the room were larger cubicles for the *surveillantes*. The washrooms at either end had their own watchdogs. No talking was allowed of course, either in the dormitory or the washrooms, where we each had an enamel bowl and a can of water. These were placed on a shelf running all the way round the room, so that we decently faced the wall as we washed. This had somehow to be achieved under one's dressing-gown, so that not an inch of bare flesh could be seen. A *surveillante* stood in the centre of the room to make sure that no indecency (such as a dressing-gown accidentally slipping to the floor) should occur.

Friday was footbath night, which took place in an enormous low-ceilinged crypt with many pillars. Between the pillars were benches on which stood tin basins. Little worker-nuns scuttled around with cans, pouring hot water into the basins as we sat on benches in complete silence, soaking and scrubbing our feet and modestly keeping our skirts well down.

After this we all trooped off to the dining-room, still in silence, for our special Friday dinner of turnips and boiled cod.

The morning and evening wash and the Friday footbaths were the only scrubbings that most of the girls got throughout the term. I, along with five other privileged boarders, was allowed a weekly bath. This was an extra, and considered dangerous to the health. The school doctor, a very old man with a little grey tuft growing out of each ear, had to be consulted every time. 'And why, Mademoiselle, do you have such a mania for baths?' he asked me once. 'It's not normal to be so obsessed with them.' But he refused permission only once, when I had a sore throat and wheezing chest.

The refectory, another enormous room in the crypt, had no windows at all, and only a few dim light-bulbs. A long table like a horseshoe ran round the room. Plates only were laid, as our own table-silver was wrapped in our napkins and tucked away on a little shelf under the table. Everybody fussed about the food, but it seemed to me perfectly acceptable. Soup came first, then meat and bread, handed round by the worker-nuns. This was followed by a vegetable, cooked as a separate course. Finally, cheese and fruit were put on the table. Bananas had to be eaten with a spoon, peaches and pears with a knife and fork. The more senior girls (from 12 upwards) had a carafe of wine and water as part of the menu. Butter was additional and Mamma, in her kindness, had ordered it for me as an extra, but the rest of the school ate their bread dry.

After dinner we all trooped into the school chapel to say

the entire rosary on our knees, and then to bed. At six-thirty next morning we were back in the chapel for Mass, after which came a quick breakfast, then straight into our class-rooms. The form-mistress always started the day with the sentence 'Mesdemoiselles, I am ready to serve you.' Like all the other teachers, she maintained the fiction that the teaching staff were our paid servants and were there to do our bidding at all times. This was infuriating, and they knew as well as we did that nobody was fooled. Why and when this practice began I have no idea. The statement may have been true in the early Middle Ages, but by the time I was there, it was certainly a big fraud.

Two male teachers actually penetrated the establishment and taught the senior school. One was the literature master, and the other taught Greek and Latin. Each would come into a classroom flanked on either side by a couple of lay-nuns, who both sat beside him throughout the lesson. We often wondered what these old men might have got up to if left alone with us, but this was beyond the imagination of even the most knowing of my classmates.

After lunch and tea we were allowed out into the garden for half an hour when the weather was fine. Otherwise we stayed in the prep room which, as in schools all over the world, reeked of dust, ink and pencil shavings. The last half-hour before supper we spent with our form-mistress, who was preparing to take the veil. She may have had a true vocation, but we were convinced she had been disappointed in love. Seductive, with a lovely fresh face, she didn't look like someone who wanted to run away from life. She read improving books to us aloud while we daydreamed at our desks, and engaged in an insidious form of questioning about our troubles and grievances which felt to us like prying on behalf of the school authorities, and which we resented very much.

In the garden we played croquet or quoits, on what had at one time been gravel but was now dust or mud, according to the time of year. We were forbidden to gather in groups of less than four, and when only two were caught conferring together, they were sent indoors to learn a fable. Consequently it was very difficult to make friends. I tried to chum up with my next-door neighbour in the dormitory, but the only idea she had in her head was to get married in order to beget as many sons as possible, for the sole purpose of killing Germans. This, she was convinced, was her patriotic duty, and she was determined to accomplish it. Circumstances thwarted her, however, as the war came far too soon for her plan to be carried out.

Our uniform was the same winter and summer – adequate in winter but sweltering in July, which can be *very* hot in Paris. It consisted of a sailor suit of heavy blue serge, with a pleated skirt and black stockings. For Sundays we had the same, but in white. Navy-blue felt hats completed the ensemble.

Our gym gear had to be seen to be believed – navy-blue knickerbockers to just below the knee with, over them, a wide flounced skirt like a lampshade, banded with white, a sailor-suit blouse also banded with white, and for the head a triangular piece of cloth tied up in front like a turban, into which all one's hair had to be tucked. Decked out in these incredible togs, we marched round and round the footbath room, from which the benches had been removed. The gym nun, whose teeth kept falling out so that she constantly had to catch them in her handkerchief, clapped her hands together as we marched. And that was our gym lesson.

Gloom and depression settled on me that term and bored their way into my spirits, which had never been so low before. It was not only the fact that nothing interesting ever happened, but also the constant watching and supervision, and the knowledge that we were all suspected of lying and cheating whenever we could.

Christmas was a dismal failure. Mamma had left with Christine for Malaya after delivering us to our various schools, and though it was a joy to see Marie and John and Anne again (all of them even more miserable than I was), the Villa Pépé was cold and gloomy beyond belief. Poor Marie, who missed Christine dreadfully, did her best to raise our spirits, but she was too low herself to do any of us much good. The Darlanges stayed in Paris, so we were alone in St Georges. We went for listless walks, and quarrelled incessantly. We would really have been much happier in Vence, and I can't think why it didn't occur to Marie to take us there. The only bright spot during the holidays was Kipling's *Captains Courageous*, which I received as a Christmas present and which transported me far, far away into a completely different world. I read it three times before going back to school.

Then suddenly, one wonderful day in early spring, a

telegram arrived from Malaya, ordering me to take a boat to England without delay. As I later discovered, it was dear Mrs Hillier who was behind this move. It was high time, she had written to Mamma, that Anne and I went to an English school, since no proper education existed outside England. Mamma, who had no trouble in accepting the idea, acted at once. I imagined her instantly writing the telegram and dispatching the estate postman with it on his bicycle.

So Anne and I were sent to Rosemead, in Littlehampton, as boarders. Our new school was a revelation. The relaxed relationship between the staff and girls never ceased to amaze me. When my desk neighbour once said in a geography lesson, 'Oh, Miss Stewart, you *are* a pig!' I nearly fell off my chair.

And then we were *trusted*. It was always assumed we would speak the truth. Another amazing fact was the spirit of co-operation that reigned between staff and pupils. The teachers were tolerantly regarded as brain boxes with a tiresome job to do, and the girls ran the school. It was the prefects and the 'subs' who organized games, outings, walks, runs and rehearsals, who assembled the school for prayers and who devised and enforced punishment for breaking the rules. 'Walking round the cabbage patch' for half an hour was one of their favourites, as it was healthy exercise and kept you out of doors, while the culprit could be watched from the dining-room windows.

There was a girl called Anne Sainsbury, half-French like us, who had the great good fortune to be able to put her back out by bending down and touching her toes. Whenever she wanted to avoid anything tiresome like church or a spell around the cabbage patch, she would surreptitiously slip away, touch her toes and come back crowing 'I've done it again!' She would then retire to the sanatorium for a couple of days with a bundle of books from the library and a pocketful of tuck. We very much envied her this useful talent. During the war Anne was to distinguish herself by her heroic work with the French Resistance, and once, when shot in that back of hers, she stoically submitted to the extraction of the bullet without anaesthetic. She was in my sister Anne's form, and they were great friends.

Unbelievably, the gates at Rosemead were open at all times, and we were allowed out into the town, in groups of three. There was no censoring of mail, and we could write to anybody we liked. It was like seeing the world upside-down. The greatest treat of all was being allowed to have as many baths as we liked. So I went overboard, with a quick dip in the morning before breakfast and a blissfully long soak later after games. And nobody ever said a word about it!

There were two headmistresses, 'Toby' who taught divinity and 'Nita' who took English literature in the sixth form. As a great treat I was allowed to attend her lessons while I was still in the fifth and for the first time I realized that Milton was not the pompous bore I had always thought him to be. All the teachers were friendly and had a sense of humour and a refreshingly detached attitude. That year I really took to Latin and Greek, which so impressed the heads that a special classics master was brought over from Lewes to teach me. We worked in Toby's drawing-room, and romped through Sophocles and Plato, Virgil and Julius Caesar. My teacher seemed to enjoy the lessons as much as I did.

Some of Rosemead's habits remained strange to me until the end. For instance, the girls always drew their cubicle curtains before saying their prayers, which to me, used to kneeling in the dust in public as I was, seemed curious to say the least, particularly as they were happy to strip to the skin and expose their naked bodies to one another without the slightest qualm. I soon learnt to say my own prayers behind drawn curtains too, but never, *never* was I able to undress in front of the others.

Another thing that has remained incomprehensible to me to this day was the effect produced by the King's abdication, which swept over the school as if an unimaginable catastrophe had occurred. Girls sobbed on their beds all afternoon, and the head girl, a vast mountain of flesh who terrified everyone on the lacrosse field, wept loudest of all, and cancelled all games for that day. Such was their grief that some of them could not even eat their evening cornflakes and I, the stony-hearted frog, dry-eyed and puzzled beyond words, gobbled up several extra suppers. It seemed to me no tragedy that the gentle-faced new King should take over a job which his brother so obviously detested. Had there been murder or foul play as, for instance, in *Macbeth*, that of course would have been a different matter.

* * *

Halfway through our career at Rosemead, Mamma suddenly decided to bring Christine back from Malaya to expose her to the civilizing influence of Europe. Bright, active, quick-witted, as ignorant as the usual run of Fesq children but far more enterprising than we had ever been at her age, and unrestrained by the fierce and ever-watchful Marie, in Malaya Christine had lived a life of total freedom. Nimble as a wild-cat, she could run up a coconut tree as well as any of the native children, whom she had dragooned into a well-disciplined army which she marched around the plantation, training them in jungle warfare and survival. Herons and other birds, killed in full flight with well-aimed stones, were roasted on camp fires which spread underground along the infinite network of dead roots, creating an appalling risk of forest fires. So, what with one thing and another, the time had come for poor Christine to be tamed.

They arrived at Christmas, and Mamma rented a small house two minutes' away from the school. The idea was that we should live there with her and Marie and go to school every morning after breakfast. This, we knew, was meant as a treat, but by then we thoroughly enjoyed boarding-school life and hated the thought of being day-girls. Neither Anne nor I ever discussed this, though we both knew what the other was thinking, but of course it was impossible to mention it to Mamma. The dreary little house she had rented, full of anti-macassars and art nouveau lampshades, had one redeeming feature – a piano in the drawing-room. So her musical evenings were resumed, and those who could sing joined in heartily. John, who had managed his affairs remarkably well, had found his way to a very easy-going, happy-go-lucky cramming establishment run by a foreign baron in Arundel. This suited us all, as he could come home whenever he liked, during the week as well as at weekends.

That winter I caught a cold which dragged on for weeks. One evening, as I was coughing over my homework in Marie's sitting-room, she suddenly said, 'I'm sure you've got TB. It's not normal to go on and on like this.'

I stared at her in alarm. 'Isn't that a deadly disease?'

'It certainly is,' she replied. 'I've seen hundreds of cases in Switzerland, coming over to be cured. Lovely girls from all over the world, coughing their lungs out, all dead within a year. Nothing you can do about it.'

My insides turned over. 'You mean that I shall be dead within a year?'

'Most likely. Mind you, it's a painless death. They even say the worse you get, the happier you feel.'

This was no consolation at all. My spirits plummeted. 'Never mind,' said Marie, as she saw me drooping. 'We all have to die sooner or later, and I will lay you out myself, and let nobody else touch you. My mother taught me how to do it, and she learnt it from *her* mother. Nowadays people don't bother any more. They let total strangers lay out their dead.' And, unconscious of her pun, she added, 'It's a dying art.'

That night I cried myself to sleep at the thought of having to die so soon, and I spent the next few days in terror of eternal damnation. But gradually the cough cleared up and my usual health and appetite returned, thereby robbing poor Marie of her treat. In fact she never had the chance to lay any of us out.

19

Towards the end of the summer term Mamma announced that we were going for the holidays to St Georges. Papa would be coming back on leave and we would meet him at the station in Marseilles as usual. Those continental railway stations in the days of steam had something which, once experienced, could never be forgotten. As we clanked into one at dead of night, with a great rattling of brakes and couplings and the screech of released steam, Marie would spring to her feet, straining out of the window to sniff the sulphurous fumes rolling slowly beneath the roof. She would then summon the trolley men, buy ham sandwiches, great slabs of Swiss chocolate, and fresh supplies of white pillows. All these were handed up to her through the window, then chucked into our waiting arms. Dogs howled, and small children whined as they were dragged along the platform, followed by tough-looking porters belted into their tunics like Russian moujiks.

On this occasion, having left his ship at Port Said, my father and a couple of friends had bought a boat and had been sailing round the Greek islands for the past three months. As the train drew into Marseilles, our excitement swelled to fever-pitch. We could hardly believe that such an arrangement would work yet again. But there, on the platform, to our delight and amazement, stood my father, aloof, patient and remote as a resigned and elderly camel. Chocolate brown from the tropical sun and his three months' sailing round the Mediterranean, he looked unfamiliar, and we were seized by our usual fit of shyness at seeing him again after several years.

When we arrived in Royan next morning, we found Jacques and his father waiting for us. They had brought their own cars and prudently booked several taxis, knowing from experience how much luggage there was likely to be. We hadn't seen our friends for a couple of years, and since then Jacques had grown at least a foot. He looked like an Olympic athlete in training. He gave me a bear-hug which squeezed the air out of my lungs, and which I bore without protest. I realized how much I had missed him, and what bliss it was to be back.

As soon as we arrived at Villa Cobalt, our new summer residence, Jacques grabbed me by the hand and we raced to the beach where we flopped down in the dunes under the tamarisk trees. For a while we sat in silence, filled with utter peace and contentment. I looked around quickly to see if anything had changed – at the cove where the fishermen let down their nets, at the reef uncovered by the retreating tide, at the diving contraption which had nearly broken my neck, and at the huge sweep of white sand stretching all the way to Suzac. No, nothing had changed. But it seemed that I had.

'You look different,' said Jacques accusingly.

'That's all the worry about exams. Lines and wrinkles,' and I smiled to show that, though wizened, I still *felt* the same.

'Anyway, you've changed too.'

'I expect you'll look better when you're brown,' he said presently.

'That won't take long,' I said, and we sat in silence, chewing the juicy ends of some grass stems.

'There's such a lot I want to tell you,' he said after a while.

'Well, there's plenty of time.'

'Yes, there's plenty of time. Let's go and help Marie with the unpacking now,' I said. 'It's not fair to leave it all to her.'

'Helping' Marie meant that Jacques sat on one of the beds, shunting the odd trunk out of the way or heaving a new one forward, into which Marie and I dived, emerging with armfuls of sheets and towels, blankets, linen hats, bathing things, first-aid kit, card games and all the paraphernalia indispensable to a well-run seaside holiday.

Villa Cobalt, directly opposite Châlet Gaudin (which was by now completely engulfed by the tangled vegetation of the garden, and very decrepit), was as bare as all the summer villas we had ever occupied, but less smelly, as the 'convenience' had a little hut all to itself in the back yard. The front garden, shaded by mulberry trees, became our studio, where we spent all our time when not on the beach or writing and illustrating our stories. During that summer holiday we discovered Katherine Mansfield's short stories, which Jacques read aloud, and when we had come to the end of her output, somebody produced Rosamond Lehmann's *Dusty Answer*, and for weeks we fell under her spell.

To supplement my pocket-money of 3 francs a week, I put

a card in the local tobacconist's advertising English lessons, to try to catch a few holiday students. This brought me several pupils and became a modestly lucrative occupation. But it swallowed up two hours every morning and elicited a great deal of grumbling from Jacques, who told me I was wasting the best time of the day in this useless way. We started at 8 a.m. as we were all (pupils and teacher alike) keen to get finished as early as possible. One morning, as we sat by an open window toiling with our 'ths' and aitches, a pebble hit me in the small of the back.

I guessed that Jacques had arrived and, turning round, saw him standing in the garden, immensely tall and golden brown, square-shouldered and grey-eyed, and quite unconscious of his looks. Suddenly I realized how lucky I was, how much I would miss his solid and reassuring presence, which even made itself felt in his letters, if he were suddenly to disappear. And there and then I made a vow to bear with his moods and his possessiveness, and never to be impatient or uncooperative again. I made a face and said, 'Nearly ready. Won't be long,' and finished the lesson in a new kind of glow. Behind me I heard him crunching back and forth on the gravel, whistling through his teeth, trying to be patient. When I finally joined him outside, he was in a surprisingly sunny mood. 'You gave me a lovely smile just then,' he said.

'Really?' This *was* unexpected! 'Don't I always smile when I see you?'

'There are smiles and smiles,' he said darkly, and went all gloomy again. I never seemed able to say the right thing. We trudged off to the beach in silence, and it was a relief to find the others already there, giggling over a game of Hangman. A great number of small cousins were there too, squabbling and rolling about in the sand. My new-found glow of loving-kindness was already wearing off as I watched Jacques stumping down to the sea to bathe, knowing by the way he walked that he was in a black rage again. Would we never be able to understand each other?

It was not until a long time afterwards, when it was much too late, that I perceived the cause of our malaise. He wanted me to grow up and enter into an adult relationship with him, a natural wish considering that I was 18 by then; but, immature and backward to an incredible degree, and mulishly clinging to the world of childhood, the last thing I wanted was to grow up. And so we were hardly ever able to tune in to the same wavelength.

* * *

The summer weather went on and on, and I loved getting up early when the sun, coming up over Suzac at the far end of the bay, slanted through the morning haze, and the garden was stretching itself awake, with buds opening up and petals unfurling. Dew-soaked grasses raised their heads as the heavy drops evaporated, spiders tightened their slackened webs, and early birds pounced on worms. It was exhilarating at that hour of the day to sniff the heady scent of the damp soil, herbs, plants and trees all around.

We went for long walks through the woods, vineyards and fields, and along the sea-shore where the beach, starting at the Spanish border, reached uninterruptedly northwards for hundreds of miles almost as far as the English Channel. And behind the dunes we came across flocks of sheep and goats with shepherds, cloaked and hooded in long brown capes, who moved around among the trees on stilts, stalking the land like Frankenstein. The great trees creaked and groaned in the sea winds, and the smell of resin oozing from their bark filled the air. Sometimes we took sandwiches, or else we stopped at a farm for bread and cheese, and (behind Mamma's back) great jugs of cider which made our legs wobble. And when we finally got home at dusk, we were loaded with mushrooms, wounded birds for Marie to heal, giant sea-shells and sharks' teeth or dogfish eggs.

On one occasion Jacques, Nadia, John and I went camping on a small deserted beach where, under the overhanging cliff, protected from the Atlantic winds and facing the rising sun, we pitched our tents. We caught crayfish and cooked them for our supper, then lay down on our bellies by the fire and made up stories, each of us adding a paragraph according to inspiration, for what seemed like hours. Finally, when my eyes would stay open no longer, I said I was going to bed, but Jacques pulled me to my feet saying, 'Let's go for one last swim.'

We slid into the smooth dark water and swam side by side for a few minutes, Jacques doing his faultless crawl while I struggled with my own version of doggy paddle. He soon outdistanced me, leaving a trail of phosphorescent froth in which I was perfectly content to roll and splash about. Apart from an infinitude of stars, the night was inky black and the water looked as if it were illuminated from below with green fluorescent light. After a while Jacques swam back and said 'lazybones' as he passed me on his way to the beach. I followed him out. He kicked sand on to the fire as he rubbed his hair and mopped his face, then we both crawled into our respective tents. Lying on our airbeds we chatted for a while through the canvas, but I kept dropping off, until, heaving a sigh, he finally said, 'Oh, go to sleep.'

* * *

One evening at the end of summer, Mamma and the Darlange parents suddenly appeared in a station-wagon in the pine wood where we were picnicking. They looked grim. War had been declared, they said, and we must pack up and come home with them at once. *'C'est la guerre.'* It was the first time we heard these words which were to become infinitely boring to us, repeated at all times by people who seemed to relish them, and of which the English equivalent, no less boring, was 'There's a war on.'

The beginning of the war, I regret to say, made very little impact on us except insofar as it affected our own lives. Our interest in it was entirely selfish. The fact that Poland had been invaded by Hitler's armies confirmed our belief, implanted in our minds by Marie as far back as we could remember, that the Germans were a bad lot. What more could you expect? It was hard luck on the poor Poles, but how they could be helped by a world war was a profound mystery to us. It was one of those things you just had to accept, because the grown-ups, who had launched the war, said it was inevitable.

There were still three weeks to go before the Darlange family had to return to Paris. It was only Jacques who would be going back this time, while Nadia and Ninette and all the young cousins were to stay on at Nostram with their grandmother and go to our college in Royan for as long as the war lasted. As far as our family was concerned, John was to go back alone to England, to his crammer in Arundel, while Anne, Christine and I were to sign on at the college in Royan once more.

Soon after the outbreak of war the autumn rains began, as implacable as any monsoon we had ever known in Malaya. We were trapped indoors, which suited me fine, as I was perfectly happy to paint, scribble and play card games with Nadia and the rest of the gang. But Jacques prowled up and down the drawing-room until even Mamma's patience began to wear thin. She asked him to sit down and read aloud to us. The book she handed him, *Le Grand Meaulnes*, was a perfect choice, as it fitted his mood like a glove. We were all mesmerized by the story and the dreamlike world in which it is set. The remaining days of our 'last summer' were so imbued with the atmosphere of the book that it feels almost like my own autobiography when I read it again.

When school started once more, Anne, Christine and I

would call at Nostram early every morning to collect the Darlange clan. They would be in the middle of breakfast when we arrived soon after seven, crowding around the table, all talking at once with their mouths full, in a state of utter confusion. The hot, steaming room smelt of wood smoke and cocoa, with dogs cluttering up the fireplace and scarves and satchels strewn all over the floor. Anne and I hunted around trying to sort out their books and their coats, and somehow or other we managed to get them all out and on their bikes by seven-thirty, our irrevocable deadline.

Pedalling furiously down the sea-road, we battled through wind and rain, our headlights flickering on and off all the way there. Because of the war, and the number of children who had stayed behind instead of going back to Paris, school ended for us at two o'clock, after which the poor *professeurs* had to take on a second batch, who worked from two till eight at night.

By then I was in the top class, doing philosophy, with huge hairy boys of 19 and 20, all immensely polite and urbane, and there was no more fighting in the schoolyard. Instead we discussed the theories of Kant and Nietzsche, and moaned about the intricacies of physics and astronomy.

Our homework was horrific, but we soon cut it down when we realized that the teachers never had a chance to mark half of it. So we spent the afternoons sprawling in the drawing-room at home or in one of the bedrooms at Nostram, gossiping, giggling or playing our usual idiotic card games, which we invented as we went along. Without Jacques always around to nag and find fault, we were able to be as silly as we liked.

And so the days went by, the weather grew colder, and the edge of the sea became encrusted with ice. The war was beginning to make itself felt. Meat, we heard on the radio, was becoming scarce. The butchers were ordered to close every other day in an effort to cut down consumption. So, as stands to reason, everybody bought twice as much on the days when they were open. By Christmas, Marie was drying out used tea-leaves for a second brewing. Soon 'coffee' beans were made of roasted acorns. Bit by bit we settled into a war routine.

It had always been Marie's practice to cut up large lumps of scrubbing soap (*savon de Marseilles*) with cheese-wire, and we would each be given a piece of it to wash with. Made for laundry and floor-scrubbing, it invariably scorched the top layer of your face off and roughed up the skin on your hands like a cheese-grater. One day my mother, who had not really looked at any of us for some time, suddenly caught sight of my sore face and asked suspiciously, 'Why is your skin so rough? What have you been putting on it?'

'Just ordinary soap,' I answered, surprised. 'Why, what's the matter?'

'You look like a crocodile handbag,' she observed. 'You ought to start using night cream.'

Night cream indeed! I was not going to spend any of my precious pocket-money on such unnecessary stuff and it was certainly not the sort of thing Marie was likely to provide. We both conveniently forgot about it and no more was said. We went on scouring ourselves with *savon de Marseilles*, and it was not until this became one of the commodities that was in short supply, when soap all but disappeared from the shops, that our skins lost their crocodile texture and showed a marked improvement.

* * *

Jacques and his parents arrived on Christmas Eve with some Belgian cousins who had foreseen the coming disaster, in spite of the government's repeated assurances that the Germans would never cross the Maginot Line. The cousins took over Châlet Gaudin which, because of its crumbling condition, was the last available house in St Georges, for the village was now filled to overflowing with refugees from the north.

We all gave a hand with painting and wall-papering, and John performed wonders on the woodwork with his hammer and fret-saw and all the other complicated and nameless tools which by now he used with professional dexterity, and by the end of the Christmas holidays Châlet Gaudin was a very desirable residence indeed. It was a strange feeling to be back in our first St Georges villa with all its memories, and now we had an extra port of call for playing cards, or reading aloud, or painting and writing.

One night when we had all gone to bed, and I was snuggling under my eiderdown and a pile of coats (the weather was fiercely cold, there was no heating in the room, and I always kept my window wide open), a shower of pebbles suddenly rattled on to the bedroom floor. Then I heard a low whistle. I struggled into one of the coats and padded over to the window. The night was bright as tempered steel, and the moon, like a white Camembert cheese against the Prussian blue of the sky, gave an eerie light, so diffused that it cast no shadows. Jacques, who had come for a late-night chat, was standing beneath my window all swaddled up in an enormous muffler. I leaned out and said hello, and how nice of him to come, but he mustn't stay as it was so very cold. This did not go down well, and he went silent, leaning against the wall and scuffing the ground with one foot. I cursed myself, but could find nothing else to say. It was desperately cold, and I longed for him to go. It would only mean another sore throat, a bad chest and a week in bed. Oh, why didn't he go? A little moan escaped me.

'What did you say?' He looked up sharply.

There was another long silence. Suddenly he said, 'You'll be ready at six?'

'Heavens! I'll never manage to wake up. It's nearly midnight now.'

'So it is. Well, I'll come round and throw gravel at your window. Please don't be late. I don't want to miss the sunrise!'

'Okay. Goodnight,' I said firmly.

'Goodnight, and you will be quick in the morning, won't you?'

I felt as if I'd hardly dropped off to sleep when the dreaded shower of gravel was pattering on to my floor again. I struggled into consciousness, scrambled into my clothes and boots, and tried to wash my face, but gave up when I realized that the water was frozen solid in the jug. Quickly brushing my hair, I screwed it into a tight knot which I skewered to my skull with all the pins I could find. As we still had no mirrors in our rooms, there was no point in even trying to titivate. Creeping through the sleeping house, I grabbed my cloak from the coat-stand in the hall and slipped outside, where Jacques was waiting for me.

'You've been ages,' he said. 'We'll have to hurry if we want to catch the sun before it comes up. Come on, let's go,' and grabbing my arm, he dragged me through the gate and out on to the cliff path, taking such huge strides that I had to break into a brisk trot to keep up with him.

We covered about five miles at this pace, and by the time we reached the high dune we were making for I was breathless, exhausted, famished and wondering whether it was really worth all the effort. However, we made it in time. The sandy hillock on which we stood was planted with young pines and the tall grass all round, frozen stiff, stuck out of the ground like knife blades. Standing still and puffing out little plumes of frosted air, we stared expectantly at the orange horizon.

The colour gradually mounted in the sky, illuminating little specks of cloud and spilling on to the wet sand and mud-flats of the bay. The sea was miles out and the tide was still retreating. Flocks of waders picked their way delicately about in the ooze; there were plovers, curlews and avocets, and another flock on tall matchstick legs, as large as storks, which even Jacques could not identify. The sky changed gradually to geranium red, and then deep ox-blood, and the sun rose slowly out of the sea. Jacques heaved a great sigh. It really meant a great deal to him to be present at this daily ascent of the sun, almost as if he didn't trust it to do the job properly without his personal supervision.

'Better than any painting in the world, isn't it, little one?' he said. I *loathed* being called 'little one', but let it pass.

'Well yes, I suppose so,' I said, but secretly I thought his own creations rather better. He got a great variety of colour into his paintings, and branched out into lovely streaks of lime and primrose which a real sunrise seldom produces. We stood still as the sun slowly climbed out of the sea and the colour faded in the sky.

'One day we'll build a hut here on this dune, and we'll live like hermits, right away from the world,' he said. 'I'll chop down trees' – he waved at the saplings around us – 'and we'll have huge log fires. I'll fish, and shoot rabbits and wild duck, and you'll make clothes for us out of their skins.'

Duck skin? Unnerved by the cold, I felt a ghastly fit of giggles coming on. Mercifully, I managed to suppress it.

Carried away by his vision, Jacques put his hand on my hair and started to poke about in it. The pins began to rain down the back of my neck and on to my face, and the wind caught my loosened hair. I gritted my teeth, but said nothing. He saw my expression and looked contrite, but it was too late.

'Let's go back before you catch cold,' he said solicitously. 'We'll cut across the fields.'

The 'fields' – a euphemism for what was normally bog-land

into which you sank hip-deep – were now frozen into ruts and troughs over which we staggered and stumbled, disturbing volleys of snipe and flocks of teal and mallard. We crossed a frozen pond, and a slow creaking sound, beginning by the sedges, ran all along the edge and a long crack appeared in the ice.

'Run for it!' shouted Jacques. 'Quick, or we'll sink.' We belted across as the ice slowly began to dip on our side. One enormous leap (M. Dupont's early training came in useful here) and we were on firm, crusty bog-land again.

'You realize that if we'd gone under we would have drowned, don't you?' Jacques said, as if I were responsible for our near-miss.

Everyone was in the drawing-room of the Villa Falaise when we returned from our expedition, and wondering what to do with the rest of the day.

'Shall we go to Royan and have tea at the pâtisserie?' suggested Nadia.

'No, it's too expensive. I've no money left this week,' said someone else.

'Let's go and see Yolande then, she's always good for a slap-up tea.'

'We've seen her three days running. Let's think of something else.'

'Let's go skating,' drawled Robert, the laziest of the Belgian cousins. He was reclining in an armchair with his feet up on the chimneypiece. We all stared at him unbelievingly, and he was already regretting his suggestion.

'Yes,' shouted everybody, 'we'll go to old Goddard's pond.'

Jacques slapped a book down on the table and stormed out of the drawing-room.

* * *

It was a cheerful, noisy crowd that skated on Goddard's pond that afternoon – until, that is, old Père Goddard himself, attracted by the noise, arrived and ordered us off, shouting that there were too many of us, and he hadn't given permission for 'the whole village to turn up and trample his crops'. Jacques's face was like thunder all the way home, and I kept well away. When we reached Nostram, however, he thawed a little and said, 'Come in and have tea. You needn't go home yet,' and he generously included John and Anne in the invitation.

Nine small faces were munching in silence around the vast dining-room table. This silence, so unexpected from the usually tumultuous small fry, surprised us considerably. It turned out later that they had all been sickening for measles, and the poor things spent the rest of their holidays in bed in the dark, lest they should go blind.

We went to the sideboard and helped ourselves to cocoa and cake, and large slices of rye bread and butter. Pots of honey and blackberry jelly were dotted about the table. A dozen or so gun-dogs lay in front of the fireplace, with their noses in the ashes. We squeezed in among the ailing ones, and Nadia described our adventures of the afternoon. Her grandmother, serene and composed, sat at one end of the table, while facing her was the other old lady of the house, who had been somebody's godmother in the distant past. Fluttering and dainty and full of little exclamations, she had lived with the family for as long as anyone could remember. With only two live-in domestics, these two ladies between them ran the house, which sometimes sheltered up to thirty beating hearts, not counting the dogs.

With markedly less enthusiasm than usual, the young cousins nibbled their slices of bread and honey. Sitting beside Jacques and watching them, I felt a great surge of love for them all, right down to the infamous 2-year-old Antoine (who, when annoyed with someone, lurked around until they had gone for a swim, then peed in their shoes). The feeling was so overpowering it made my chest positively ache, and I put my hand on Jacques's knee. Unused to such demonstrations of affection, he turned in surprise. 'Are you all right?' he asked anxiously.

'Yes, quite all right, but I think we ought to go.'

He walked back with us, and we sang '*Malbrouk s'en va-t-en guerre*' all the way home as we crunched along the frozen beach under the moonlit sky.

* * *

Jacques and I continued our sunrise expeditions, not abandoning them even in gale conditions. One morning, when we reached our sand dune, with the wind lashing around us like a whip, the sun having duly risen, Jacques said: 'Let's get into that hollow. It should be more sheltered there.'

We jumped into a kind of sandy bunker at the foot of a great pine tree which creaked and groaned all the way down its trunk like the mast of a ship. Out of the wind it was really quite warm, a real little sun-trap and as cosy as could be. Woodpigeons, annoyed at being blown out of their trees, complained persistently, while lapwings and plovers pecked around us like domestic fowl.

'Why don't you lie down?' Jacques said. 'We can do a bit of sunbathing,' and we stretched out side by side. It was delicious. I closed my eyes and basked luxuriously.

Suddenly and without warning he bent over and kissed me. I sat up with a jolt, and our foreheads met with a clash, like fighting stags. Taken by surprise, I leapt up. 'How dare you trick me like that!' I shouted at him, with tears of rage pouring down my face. 'Now you've spoilt everything!'

It was a very sullen walk home, and I refused to speak to him for the rest of the day. He had indeed spoilt everything. After that I was on my guard and wouldn't go for walks with him any more. Poor John, whom he bored to death with his miseries, finally came to me and said, 'For God's sake, can't you be decent to him again? Aren't you making a lot of fuss about nothing? What's wrong with a kiss anyway?'

'It's not the kissing so much as the way he did it. He tricked me. It was a mean thing to do,' I said, still upset. But eventually I allowed him to resume our old companionship – on the absolute condition that there would be no more soppy stuff – and we went on our walks along the sea-shore again.

20

With the coming of spring, suddenly and without warning, came the beginning of the end. The first blow leading to the complete collapse of France was dealt on 10 May, with the invasion of Belgium. This trap, craftily laid by the Germans, worked perfectly. The British Expeditionary Force, backed by the First and Seventh Armies, swept forward to the defence of Belgium. This made it possible for the Panzer divisions, breaking through on the River Meuse where least expected, to surprise the Allied forces from behind, surrounding them and splitting the French army in half.

I am still convinced that the fall of France in 1940 was brought about by the same attitudes that had caused her defeat at Agincourt. The knights of the time, once safely in their armour, thought themselves invincible. In the same way, the French army of 1940 didn't realize that, with its slow-moving tanks and other outdated equipment, it was no longer able to deal with the fast-moving, up-to-date methods of the enemy. Relying on the so-called impregnability of the Maginot Line and still thinking in terms of trench warfare, the French High Command were completely taken by surprise by the lightning attack of the Panzer divisions. Having burst through the defences, they thundered towards the sea, mowing down any opposition in their path. Too late, the Allied forces in Belgium realized what had happened, and Hitler announced triumphantly that he had fooled the West.

Calais fell on 26 May, and the next day Churchill ordered the evacuation of the BEF. The world held its breath during the next nine days, while under fierce bombing from the Luftwaffe, 338,000 men embarked in the numberless craft of every kind that came sailing to their rescue from England, and the miracle of Dunkirk was accomplished. At the time we didn't believe a word of all this, assuming it to be a story put out by the government to boost the country's morale.

On 10 June came the 'stab in the back', when Mussolini declared war on France. We were then told by the French Government that there would be 'fighting to the last' at the Somme and Aisne rivers. When these battles were lost, organized resistance was over and Paris was declared an open city. After that the Germans spread out in all directions. On 13 June, when Churchill flew to France unexpectedly, the French Prime Minister asked to be let off his undertaking not to make a separate peace with Germany.

By then, thousands of refugees were flooding through St Georges, day and night, bringing with them fresh stories of the latest captured towns, and of German fighters dive-bombing and machine-gunning the endless crowds trudging south along the French roads. We offered to help, and soon found ourselves in charge of the Citizens' Advice Bureau, handing out blankets and cups of coffee, and trying to find sleeping quarters for the homeless thousands. People who had been machine-gunned on their long journey south arrived pushing prams stuffed with saucepans and suitcases and exhausted scruffy babies. Lines of cars and horse-drawn carts, loaded with wardrobes, armchairs and potted plants, moved slowly along the streets, and nowhere could food or petrol be found. Wounded soldiers bandaged with dirty, blood-stained rags hobbled in, begging for aspirin and brandy. They had long ago lost their regiments and they said the enemy were sweeping through the land at unbelievable speed.

Marie, who 'knew' the Germans, said they would rape the girls at once, and we must all wear glasses and scrape our hair back in rubber bands, then hide in the attic for extra safety. Nadia and Ninette, with their smooth brown faces and flirting eyes, were considered to be in greatest danger, although even Anne and I, straight-haired and scrawny though we were, need not think ourselves safe. As my sole acquaintance with this fate was through the story of the Rape of the Sabine Women, the whole idea seemed fantastically unreal.

When the loudspeaker in the market square announced that the Panzer divisions had reached La Rochelle, poor Mamma, who was quite distracted, went to ask the Mayor's advice. 'Get out!' he shouted at her. 'Get out immediately. I will give you all the petrol you want as long as you go. I don't want any British around when the Germans arrive.' Following the well-laid plans of the German propaganda machine, fifth-columnists had been spreading panic with claims that *les Boches* were shooting all British civilians on sight.

And so Jacques' father, collecting our petrol ration from the town hall, offered to drive us to Le Verdon across the estuary, where a British destroyer now lay at anchor, waiting to gather up any stray Britons still left on French soil. At eleven in the morning, just as we were about to leave, the destroyer was struck by a torpedo, and sank from sight within half an hour. There was only once place left to go, and that was Bordeaux, where the British Consul would take us under his wing. Jacques was to come with us to London, where he would join the Free French forces of Colonel de Gaulle.

And now comes the most painful part of the story. Mamma announced that only British subjects with British passports would be repatriated to England. And so Marie, with her Swiss passport, would have to be left behind. We were thunderstruck. In a fury of grief we turned on our mother and said many things which I, for one, much regretted later. We were no better, I told her bitterly, than a bunch of rats leaving a sinking ship; our duty was to stay on and carry out as much sabotage as we could until the Germans were finally defeated, and leaving Marie behind was the basest deed ever perpetrated by any human being. The fact that Mamma had arranged for Marie to go and live at Nostram with the Darlange family didn't improve the situation in any way. Marie's home was with us and no one else – not even our dearly beloved friends.

As none of us could swallow anything, Marie made us a packet of sandwiches, and we piled into the Darlange car, all of us sobbing helplessly. Throughout the afternoon we inched along the road to Bordeaux in bottom gear, hemmed in on all sides by thousands of refugees, fleeing they knew not where.

The noise and the heat, with the scorching June sun blazing down on us, were almost unbearable. As we could take no luggage, Mamma had insisted we all wear two sets of clothing and we sweltered, while Christine, who was still not 8, howled all the way for Marie. Dusk fell without the faintest breeze, and the heat wave continued throughout the night. Altogether it was as near a nightmare as real life could ever be.

On the edge of a small village whose name – St-André-de-Cubzac – I shall never forget, the car came to a halt and refused to go any further. Leaving it by the roadside, we walked to the *auberge* at the entrance to the village. The *patronne*, who was astonishingly affable, said yes, we could spend the night in her attic, if we didn't mind sleeping on the floor, or object to mice, rats and owls. This sounded to us like paradise. It was well after midnight when we toiled up the attic stairs, while Mamma tried to wheedle a loaf of bread out of the management. But there was no food to be had, even at black-market prices, and apart from a few plums we managed to buy in the morning we had to go hungry for the next three days.

We rushed to the wide-open attic window, which framed the distant spectacle of a burning town. Bordeaux was on fire. Christine, who was so tired she had only just managed the stairs, gripped the window-sill and jumped up and down with excitement. 'Look,' she cried, leaning out and balancing on her middle to get a better view, 'Fireworks! Lovely fireworks!' Clutching her by the waist, I dragged her back. From where we stood, we had a clear view of the raid on the town.

Sweeping in circles, the German bombers, lit up from below, looked like gigantic fireflies among the exploding bombs.

'Oh dear God,' Jacques groaned. 'What are we going to do? Whatever is going to become of us?'

I looked at his uncomprehending face, and thought of our great-grandfathers who had so confidently set out over a hundred years ago from the town which was now blazing like a jungle fire. I thought of Marie, abandoned to her most hated enemy in her old age, of the thousands of homeless people all over the country frantically fleeing from the invading armies. And I knew that whatever was to become of us, it was going to be *our* war, in which we would soon have to play our part. And that our childhood was over for ever.